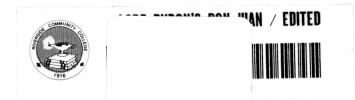

Modern Critical Interpretations

Lord Byron's
Don Juan

Modern Critical Interpretations

These and other titles in preparation

Modern Critical Interpretations

Lord Byron's
Don Juan

Edited and with an introduction by
Harold Bloom
Sterling Professor of the Humanities
Yale University

Chelsea House Publishers ◇ *1987*

NEW YORK ◇ NEW HAVEN ◇ PHILADELPHIA

© 1987 by Chelsea House Publishers, a division of Chelsea
House Educational Communications, Inc.,
   95 Madison Avenue, New York, NY 10016
   345 Whitney Avenue, New Haven, CT 06511
   5014 West Chester Pike, Edgemont, PA 19028

Introduction © 1987 by Harold Bloom

Printed and bound in the United States of America

∞ The paper used in this publication meets the minimum
requirements of the American National Standard for Permanence
of Paper for Printed Library Materials, Z39.48–1984.

Library of Congress Cataloging-in-Publication Data
Lord Byron's Don Juan.
   (Modern critical interpretations)
   Bibliography: p.
   Includes index.
   1. Byron, George Gordon Byron, Baron, 1788–1824.
Don Juan.   2. Don Juan (Legendary character) in
literature.   I. Bloom, Harold.   II. Series.
PR4359.L6   1987   821'.7   86–29973
ISBN 0–87754–733–5

ontents

Editor's Note

This book gathers together a representative selection of the best criticism devoted to Lord Byron's Romantic comic epic poem, *Don Juan*. The critical essays are reprinted here in the chronological order of their original publication. I am grateful to Wendell Piez for his work as a researcher for this volume.

My introduction, an overview of the entire, vast but unfinished poem, centers upon the dialectical interplay of Byron's neoclassic satire and his High Romantic sensibility. George Ridenour begins the chronological sequence with his powerful description of the theological context of *Don Juan,* which can be called post-Calvinist or post-Jansenist, and which never allows us, for very long, to forget the Fall of Man and its consequences.

The form of *Don Juan* is examined by Jerome J. McGann, who finds in the poem Byron's pragmatic exemplification of the stance he wishes Romantic poetry to take towards itself. Peter J. Manning explores Juan as a self-representation of Byron's own ongoing boyhood, while Michael G. Cooke studies the critical issue of the poem's apparent spontaneity.

In a shrewd but disputable reading, Candace Tate sees the poem as Byron's psychodrama, with Juan not as the hero, but as the representation of a man in a frenzy. The grand shipwreck of canto 2 of the poem is the subject of Andrew M. Cooper, who properly ends this book with a consideration of what may be Byron's leading trait, his profound skepticism.

Introduction

On the back of his manuscript of canto 1 of *Don Juan*, Byron scribbled an exemplary stanza:

> I would to heaven that I were so much clay,
>   As I am blood, bone, marrow, passion, feeling—
> Because at least the past were pass'd away—
>   And for the future—(but I write this reeling,
> Having got drunk exceedingly to-day,
>   So that I seem to stand upon the ceiling)
> I say—the future is a serious matter—
> And so—for God's sake—hock and soda-water!

The empirical world of *Don Juan* is typified in this stanza. The poem is identifiable with Byron's mature life, and excludes nothing vital in that life, and so could not be finished until Byron was. *Don Juan*'s extraordinary range of tone is unique in poetry, but Byron's was a unique individuality, preeminent even in an age of ferocious selfhood.

Don Juan began (September 1818) as what Byron called simply "a poem in the style and manner of *Beppo,* encouraged by the success of the same." But as it developed, the poem became something more ambitious, a satire of European Man and Society which attempts epic dimensions. In the end the poem became Byron's equivalent to Wordsworth's projected *Recluse,* Blake's *Milton,* Shelley's *Prometheus,* and Keats's *Hyperion*. As each of these attempts to surpass and, in Blake's and Shelley's poems, correct Milton, so Byron also creates his vision of the loss of Paradise and the tribulations of a fallen world of experience. There is no exact precedent for an epic satire of this kind. Byron's poetic idol was Pope, who kept his finest satiric strain for *The Dunciad* and

1

wrote his theodicy, without overt satire, in the *Essay on Man*. Had Pope tried to combine the two works in the form of an Italianate medley or mock-heroic romance, something like *Don Juan* might have resulted. Pope's major work is his *Essay on Man, Dunciad, Rape of the Lock,* and a good deal more besides. Where Byron falls below his Augustan Master in aesthetic genius, he compensates by the range of his worldly knowledge, and the added complexity of bearing the burden of a Romantic Imagination he could neither trust nor eradicate. Much as he wished to emulate Pope, his epic moves in the poetic world of Wordsworth and Shelley, very nearly as much as *Childe Harold* did.

Yet he wills otherwise. The poem's most acute critic, George Ridenour, emphasizes that Byron has chosen "to introduce his longest and most ambitious work with an elaborately traditional satire in the Augustan manner." The seventeen-stanza Dedication savages Southey, Wordsworth, and Coleridge, and suggests that Byron is a very different kind of poet and man, whose faults "are at least those of passion and indiscretion, not of calculation, venality, self-conceit, or an impotence which manifests itself in tyranny," to quote Ridenour again. Byron is establishing his *persona* or dramatized self, the satirical mask in which he will present himself as narrator of *Don Juan*. Southey, Wordsworth, and Coleridge are renegades, revolutionary zealots who have become Tories. Southey indeed is an "Epic Renegade," both more venal than his friends (he is poet laureate) and an offender against the epic form, which he so frequently and poorly attempts. As laureate, he is "representative of all the race" of poets, and his dubious moral status is therefore an emblem of the low estate to which Byron believes poetry has fallen:

> And Coleridge, too, has lately taken wing,
>   But like a hawk encumber'd with his hood,—
> Explaining metaphysics to the nation—
> I wish he would explain his Explanation.

Coleridge's flight is genuine but blind. Southey's poetic soarings end in a "tumble downward like the flying fish gasping on deck." As for Wordsworth, his "rather long *Excursion*" gives a "new system to perplex the sages." Byron does not make the mistake of mounting so high, nor will he fall so low:

> For me, who, wandering with pedestrian Muses,
>   Contend not with you on the winged steed,

>   I wish your fate may yield ye, when she chooses,
>   The fame you envy, and the skill you need.

He will not attempt the sublime, and thus he need not fall into the bathetic. From Southey he passes to the Master Tory, "the intellectual eunuch Castlereagh," a pillar of the Age of Reaction that followed Napoleon, and the master of Southey's hired song:

>   Europe has slaves, allies, kings, armies still,
>   And Southey lives to sing them very ill.

The mock dedication concluded, the epic begins by announcing its hero:

>   I want a hero: an uncommon want,
>   When every year and month sends forth a new one,
>   Till, after cloying the gazettes with cant,
>   The age discovers he is not the true one:
>   Of such as these I should not care to vaunt,
>   I'll therefore take our ancient friend Don Juan—
>   We all have seen him, in the pantomime,
>   Sent to the devil somewhat ere his time.

This last may be a reference to Mozart's *Don Giovanni*. Byron's Don Juan shares only a name with the hero of the legend or of Mozart. At the root of the poem's irony is the extraordinary passivity and innocence of its protagonist. This fits the age, Byron insists, because its overt heroes are all military butchers. The gentle Juan, acted upon and pursued, sets off the aggressiveness of society.

The plot of *Don Juan* is too extensive for summary, and the poem's digressive technique would defeat such an attempt in any case. The poem organizes itself by interlocking themes and cyclic patterns, rather than by clear narrative structure. "A deliberate rambling digressiveness," Northrop Frye observes, "is endemic in the narrative technique of satire, and so is a calculated bathos or art of sinking in its suspense." *Don Juan* parodies epic form and even its own digressiveness. Its organization centers, as Ridenour shows, on two thematic metaphors: the Fall of Man, in terms of art, nature, and the passions; and the narrator's style of presentation, in terms of his rhetoric and his *persona*. Juan's experiences tend toward a cyclic repetition of the Fall, and Byron's style as poet and man undergoes the same pattern of aspiration and descent.

Canto 1 deals with Juan's initial fall from sexual innocence. The tone of this canto is urbanely resigned to the necessity of such a fall, and the description of young love and of Donna Julia's beauty clearly ascribes positive qualities to them. Yet Julia is rather unpleasantly changed by her illicit love affair, and her parting letter to Juan betrays a dubious sophistication when we contrast it to her behavior earlier in the canto. As Byron says, speaking mockingly of his own digressiveness:

> The regularity of my design
>> Forbids all wandering as the worst of sinning.

His quite conventional moral design condemns Julia, without assigning more than a merely technical lapse to the seduced sixteen-year-old, Juan. The self-baffled Prometheanism of *Childe Harold* manifests itself again here in *Don Juan,* but now the emphasis is rather more firmly set against it. "Perfection is insipid in this naughty world of ours," and Byron is not prepared to be even momentarily insipid, but the price of passion, with its attendant imperfections, may be damnation. And so Byron writes of "first and passionate love":

>> —it stands alone,
> Like Adam's recollection of his fall;
>> The tree of knowledge has been pluck'd
>> —all's known—
> And life yields nothing further to recall
>> Worthy of this ambrosial sin, so shown,
> No doubt in fable, as the unforgiven
> Fire which Prometheus filch'd for us from heaven.

Imaginatively this is an unfortunate passage, as it reduces both Man's crime and the Promethean theft from the level of disobedience, which is voluntaristic, to that of sexuality itself, a natural endowment. Byron's paradoxes concerning sexual love are shallow, and finally irksome. It is not enlightening to be told that "pleasure's a sin, and sometimes sin's a pleasure."

Byron does better when he finds Prometheanism dubiously at work in human inventiveness:

> One makes new noses, one a guillotine,
>> One breaks your bones, one sets them in their sockets.

In an age full of new inventions, "for killing bodies, and for saving souls," both alike made with great good will, the satirist finds a true function in exploring the ambiguities of human aspiration. When Byron merely condemns all aspiration as sinful, he repels us. Fortunately, he does not play Urizen for very long at a time. What is most moving in canto 1 is the final personal focus. After extensive ridicule of Coleridge and Wordsworth, Byron nevertheless comes closest to his own deep preoccupations in two stanzas that are no more than a weaker version of the "Intimations" and "Dejection" odes:

No more—no more—Oh! never more on me
  The freshness of the heart can fall like dew,
Which out of all the lovely things we see
  Extracts emotions beautiful and new;
Hived in our bosoms like the bag o' the bee.
  Think'st thou the honey with those objects grew?
Alas! 'twas not in them, but in thy power
To double even the sweetness of a flower.

This is a very naive version of the "Dejection" ode. What we receive is what we ourselves give. Byron's scorn of "metaphysics" and "system" in Coleridge and Wordsworth, which is actually a rather silly scorn of deep thought in poetry, betrays him into a very weak though moving performance in the mode of Romantic nostalgia for the innocent vision both of external and of human nature:

No more—no more—Oh! never more, my heart,
  Canst thou be my sole world, my universe!
Once all in all, but now a thing apart,
  Thou canst not be my blessing or my curse:
The illusion's gone for ever, and thou art
  Insensible, I trust, but none the worse,
And in thy stead I've got a deal of judgment,
Though heaven knows how it ever found a lodgment.

The last couplet helps the stanza, as an ironic equivalent to Wordsworth's "sober coloring" of mature vision, but the preceding lines are weak in that they recall "Peele Castle," and fall far short of it. Not that Byron is thinking of either Coleridge or Wordsworth in these two stanzas; it is more to the point to note that he might have done better to think of them, and so avoid the bathos of unconsciously, and awkwardly, suggesting their major poetic concerns.

In canto 2 Juan is sent on his travels, and suffers seasickness, shipwreck, and the second and greatest of his loves. The shipwreck affords Byron a gruesome opportunity to demonstrate fallen nature at its helpless

worst, as the survivors turn to a cannibalism that is rather nastily portrayed. From the flood of judgment only Juan is saved, for only he refrains
from tasting human flesh. He reaches shore, a new Adam, freshly bap-
tized from the waves, to find before him a new Eve, Haidée, daughter
of an absent pirate. She seems innocence personified, but for Byron no
person is innocent. Though it is an "enlargement of existence" for Haidée
"to partake Nature" with Juan, the enlargement carries with it the burden
of man's fall. Byron himself keenly feels the lack of human justice in this
association. First love, "nature's oracle," is all "which Eve has left her
daughters since her fall." Yet these moments will be paid for "in an
endless shower of hell-fire":

> Oh, Love! thou art the very god of evil,
> For, after all, we cannot call thee devil.

Canto 3 is mostly a celebration of ideal love, but its very first stanza
pictures Juan as being

> loved by a young heart, too deeply blest
> To feel the poison through her spirit creeping,
> Or know who rested there, a foe to rest,
> Had soil'd the current of her sinless years,
> And turn'd her pure heart's purest blood to tears!

This seems an equivocal deep blessing for Haidée, "Nature's bride"
as she is. Yet, Byron goes on to say, they *were* happy, "happy in the illicit
indulgence of their innocent desires." This phrasing takes away with one
hand what it gives with the other. When, in the fourth canto, all is over,
with Juan wounded and sold into slavery, and Haidée dead of a roman-
tically broken heart, Byron gives us his most deliberate stanza of moral
confusion. Haidée has just died, and her unborn child with her:

> She died, but not alone; she held within
> A second principle of life, which might
> Have dawn'd a fair and sinless child of sin;
> But closed its little being without light,
> And went down to the grave unborn, wherein
> Blossom and bough lie wither'd with one blight;
> In vain the dews of Heaven descend above
> The bleeding flower and blasted fruit of love.

This is a pathetic kind of sentimental neo-Calvinism until its concluding couplet, when it becomes a statement of the inefficacy of heavenly

grace in the affairs of human passion. At the start of the fourth canto Byron had modulated his tone so as to fit his style to the saddest section of his epic. If a fall is to be portrayed, then the verse too must descend:

> Nothing so difficult as a beginning
>   In poesy, unless perhaps the end;
> For oftentimes when Pegasus seems winning
>   The race, he sprains a wing, and down we tend,
> Like Lucifer when hurl'd from heaven for sinning;
>   Our sin the same, and hard as his to mend,
> Being pride, which leads the mind to soar too far,
> Till our own weakness shows us what we are.

Few stanzas in *Don Juan* or elsewhere are as calmly masterful as that. The poet attempting the high style is likely to suffer the fate of Lucifer. Pride goes before the fall of intellect, and the sudden plunge into bathos restores us to the reality we are. The movement from *Childe Harold* into *Don Juan* is caught with fine self-knowledge:

> Imagination droops her pinion,
> And the sad truth which hovers o'er my desk
> Turns what was once romantic to burlesque.

Self-recognition leads to a gentler statement of mature awareness than Byron usually makes:

> And if I laugh at any mortal thing,
>   'Tis that I may not weep; and if I weep,
> 'Tis that our nature cannot always bring
>   Itself to apathy, for we must steep
> Our hearts first in the depths of Lethe's spring
>   Ere what we least wish to behold will sleep:
> Thetis baptized her mortal son in Styx;
> A mortal mother would on Lethe fix.

This is noble and restrained, and reveals the fundamental desperation that pervades the world of the poem, which is our world. After the death of Haidée most of the tenderness of Byron passes out of the poem, to be replaced by fiercer ironies and a reckless gaiety that can swerve into controlled hysteria. It becomes clearer that Byron's universe is neither Christian nor Romantic, not yet the eighteenth-century cosmos he would have liked to repossess. Neither grace nor the displaced grace of the Secondary Imagination can move with freedom in this universe, and a standard of reasonableness is merely a nostalgia to be studied. What haunts Byron is the specter of meaninglessness, of pointless absurdity. He is an unwilling prophet of our sensibility. The apocalyptic desires of Blake and Shelley, the natural sacramentalism of Coleridge and Wordsworth, the humanistic naturalism of Keats, all find some parallels in Byron, but what is central in him stands apart from the other great Romantics. He lacks their confidence, as he lacks also the persuasiveness of their individual rhetorics. Too traditional to be one of them, too restless and driven to be traditional, impatient of personal myth if only because he incarnates his own too fully, he creates a poem without faith in Nature, Art, Society, or the very Imagination he so capably employs. Yet his obsessions betray his uncertainties of rejection. *Don Juan* cannot let Wordsworth alone, and cannot bring itself to mention Shelley, Byron's companion during much of the poem's composition. Until Shelley's death, Byron could not decide what to make of either the man or the poet, both of whom impressed him more than he cared to acknowledge. After Shelley's death, Byron seems to have preferred to forget him, except for one stanza of *Don Juan* where the puzzle of Shelley continues as a troubling presence:

> And that's enough, for love is vanity,
>   Selfish in its beginning as its end,
> *Except where 'tis a mere insanity,*
>   *A maddening spirit which would strive to blend*
> *Itself with beauty's frail inanity,*
>   On which the passion's self seems to depend;
> And hence some heathenish philosophers
> Make love the main-spring of the universe.

The italics are mine, and indicate the probable Shelley reference. The stanza's first two lines express the mature judgment of Byron on love, a vanity that begins and ends in selfishness, except in the case of the rare spirits who madden themselves and others by questing as though the world could contain the object of their fierce desire. The tone here is uneasy, as it is in Byron's continuous digressions on Wordsworth's *Excursion*. *The Excursion* contains just enough of Wordsworth's greatness both to influence and to repel Byron, and its emphasis on the correction of a misanthropic Solitary may have offended him directly. We cannot know, but a surmise is possible. There are moments in *Don Juan* when Byron longs to make nature his altar, and moments when he is drawn toward a desperate religion of love. His rejection of Wordsworth and evasion of Shelley have deep and mysterious roots within *Don Juan*'s underlying assumptions concerning reality.

After the love-death of Haidée, Byron moves Juan into the world of two rapacious empresses, Gulbeyaz of Turkey and the historical Catherine the Great of Russia. Between these tigresses the poem progresses by an account of a battle between Turks and Russians. After Catherine's court, *Don Juan* starts its last, most interesting and unfinished movement, a view of the English society that Byron had known before his exile. A fierce love, a faithless war, another fierce love, and a social satire of what was closest to Byron's heart form a suggestive sequence. Seduced by a young matron, shipwrecked into an idyl of natural and ideal love, wounded and sold into bondage—the passive Juan has encountered all these adventures without developing under their impact. As he falls further into experience, he does not gain in wisdom, but he does maintain a stubborn Spanish aristocratic pride and a basic disinterestedness. Turkish passion and the horror of battle do not seem to affect him directly, but the embraces of Catherine finally convert his disinterestedness into the sickness of uninterestedness. Probably, like Childe Harold and Byron, the Don begins to feel the "fulness of satiety." His diplomatic rest trip to England is a quest for a renewal of interest, and the quest's goal, Lady Adeline, becomes Byron's last vision of a possible and therefore ultimately dangerous woman. In thus patterning the course of the poem, I have moved ahead of my commentary, and return now to Juan in slavery.

The memorable elements in that episode are the digressions. With Juan pausing, involuntarily, between women, Byron is free to meditate upon the impermanence of all worldly vanities, including poetry. He is back in the mood of *Childe Harold,* from which only the therapy of his own epic can rescue him:

> Yet there will still be bards: though fame is smoke,
>   Its fumes are frankincense to human thought;
> And the unquiet feelings, which first woke
>   Song in the world, will seek what then they sought:
> As on the beach the waves at last are broke,
>   Thus to their extreme verge the passions brought
> Dash into poetry, which is but passion,
> Or at least was so ere it grew a fashion.

Poetry here is expression and catharsis, and nothing more. At most it can help keep the poet (and his readers) sane. Elsewhere in *Don Juan* Byron rates poetry as simultaneously higher and lower, when he sees it as a dangerous mode of evading the consequences of Man's Fall, an evasion that must resolve at last in the consciousness of delusion. The impermanence of poetry is related to human mortality and what lies beyond its limits. Before introducing Juan into a Turkish harem, Byron perplexes himself with the mystery of death, drawing upon "a fact, and no poetic fable." His acquaintance, the local military commandant, has been slain in the street "for some reason, surely bad." As Byron stares at the corpse, he cannot believe that this is death:

> I gazed (as oft I have gazed the same)
> To try if I could wrench aught out of death
> Which should confirm, or shake, or make a faith;
>
> But it was all a mystery. Here we are,
>   And there we go:—but *where?* five bits of lead,
> Or three, or two, or one, send very far!
>   And is this blood, then, form'd but to be shed?
> Can every element our element mar?
>   And air—earth—water—fire live—and we dead?
> *We,* whose minds comprehend all things. No more;
> But let us to the story as before.

What is effective here is the human attitude conveyed, but Byron's own turbulence weakens the expression. Few great poets have written quite so badly about death. The Muse of Byron was too lively to accommodate the grosser of his private apprehensions. The paradox of an all-comprehensive mind inhabiting a form vulnerable to every element is the basis of Byron's dualism, his own saddened version of "the ghost in the machine." The inevitable corruption of the body obsesses Byron, and his obsession determines his dismissal of passionate love as a value. Julia was self-corrupted, and Haidée the most natural and innocent of sinners, too harshly judged by her father, himself a great cutthroat but perfectly conventional in questions of his own family's morality. Gulbeyaz is further down in the scale of female culpability. Her features have "all the sweetness of the devil" when he played the cherub. She has the charm of her passion's intensity, but her love is a form of imperial, or imperious, bondage, her embrace a chain thrown about her lover's neck. Her love is a variation of war and preludes Byron's ferocious and very funny satire on the siege, capture, and sack of the Turkish town Ismail by the ostensibly Christian imperial Russian army of Catherine the Great, Juan's next and most consuming mistress. Byron introduces canto 7 and its slaughter by parodying Spenser, whose *Faerie Queene* sang of "fierce warres and faithful loves." For Byron, it is altogether too late in the day to sing so innocently, especially when "the fact's about the same," so his themes are "fierce loves and faithless wars":

> "Let there be light!" said God, "and there was light!"
>   "Let there be blood!" says man, and there's a sea!
> The fiat of this spoil'd child of the Night
>   (For Day ne'er saw his merits) could decree
> More evil in an hour, than thirty bright
>   Summers could renovate, though they should be
> Lovely as those which ripen'd Eden's fruit;
> For war cuts up not only branch, but root.

War completes the Fall of Man, costing us our surviving root in Eden and nullifying the renovating power of nature. This does not prevent Byron from an immense and sadistic joy in recording the butchery and rapine, but his *persona* as Promethean poet, whose every stanza heightens aspiration and deepens guilt, justifies the seeming inconsistency.

Juan has butchered freely, but refrained from ravishing, and next appears as hero at the court of Catherine the Great, where he falls, not into love, but into "that no less imperious passion," self-love. Flattered by Catherine's preference, Juan grows "a little dissipated" and becomes very much a royal favorite. As this is morally something of a further fall, Byron is inspired to reflect again upon his favorite theme:

> Man fell with apples, and with apples rose,
>   If this be true; for we must deem the mode
> In which Sir Isaac Newton could disclose
>   Through the then unpaved stars the turnpike road,
> A thing to counterbalance human woes:
>   For ever since immortal man hath glow'd
> With all kinds of mechanics, and full soon
> Steam-engines will conduct him to the moon.

The triumphs of reason are now also identified as sinfully and gloriously Promethean, and Sir Isaac observing the apple's fall is responsible for the paradox that Man's initial fall with apples was a fortunate one. The glowing of human intellect is "a thing to counterbalance human woes," and soon enough will take us to the moon. Byron quickly goes on to qualify this counterbalance as "a glorious glow," due only to his internal spirit suddenly cutting a caper. Cheerfulness thus keeps breaking in, but does not alter the fundamental vision of our world as "a waste and icy clime." That clime surrounds us, and we are "chill, and chain'd to cold earth," as our hero Prometheus was upon his icy rock. But we look up, and see the meteors of love and glory, lovely lights that flash and then die away, leaving us "on our freezing way." *Don Juan* is not only, its poet tells us, "a nondescript and ever-varying rhyme," but it is also "a versified Aurora Borealis," a northern light flashing over us.

Love and glory have flashed too often for Juan, and he begins to waste into a clime of decay just as his creator laments that Dante's "obscure wood," the midpoint of life, draws close. In "royalty's vast arms," Juan sighs for beauty, and sickens for travel. The now motherly Catherine sends her wasting lover on his last quest, a mission to England, and Byron returns in spirit to the Age of Elegance of his triumphant youth, the London of the Regency.

This, *Don Juan*'s last and unfinished movement, is its most nostalgic and chastened. Byron, once "the grand Napoleon of the realms of rhyme," revisits in vision his lost kingdom, the Babylon that sent him into exile and pilgrimage. "But I will fall at least as fell my hero," Byron cries, completing his lifelong comparison to the other Titan of the age. The poem of Juan, Byron says, is his Moscow, and he seeks in its final cantos his Waterloo. Juan has met his Moscow in Catherine, and evidently would have found a Waterloo in the Lady Adeline Amundeville, cold heroine of the final cantos and "the fair most fatal Juan ever met."

The English cantos are a litany for an eighteenth-century world, forever lost, and by Byron forever lamented. The age of reason and love is over, the poet insists, and the age of Cash has begun. The poem has seen sex displaced into war, and now sees both as displaced into money. Money and coldness dominate England, hypocritically masked as the morality that exiled Byron and now condemns his epic. There are other and deeper wounds to be revenged. The Greek and Italian women of the poet's life have given fully of their passion and spirits, and Byron has returned what he could. But England stands behind him as a sexual battlefield where he conquered all yet won nothing, and where at last he defeated himself and fled. Incest, separation, mutual betrayal of spirit are his English sexual legacy. In his sunset of poetry he returns to brood upon English womankind, products of "the English winter—ending in July, to recommence in August." Beneath the Lady Adeline's snowy surface is the proverbial *et caetera,* as Byron says, but he refuses to hunt down the tired metaphor. He throws out another figure: a bottle of champagne "frozen into a very vinous ice."

> Yet in the very centre, past all price,
>   About a liquid glassful will remain;
> And this is stronger than the strongest grape
>   Could e'er express in its expanded shape.

Severity and courtliness fuse here into definitive judgment, and bring the spirit of this female archetype to a quintessence:

> And thus the chilliest aspects may concentre
> A hidden nectar under a cold presence.

Adeline is mostly a cold potential in this unfinished poem; her fatality is only barely felt when Byron breaks off, in his preparation for his final and genuinely heroic pilgrimage, to battle for the Greeks. She is Byron's "Dian of the Ephesians," but there is more flesh and activity to "her frolic Grace," the amorous Duchess of Fitz-Fulke. No personage, but an atmosphere, dominates these English cantos, with their diffused autumnal tone and their perfectly bred but desperately bored aristocrats, with whose breeding and boredom alike Byron is more than half in sympathy.

Don Juan, begun as satiric epic, ends as a remembrance of things past, with Byron's last glance at home, and the poet's last tone one of weary but loving irony. The last word in a discussion of *Don Juan* ought not to be "irony," but "mobility," one of Byron's favorite terms. Oliver Elton called Byron's two central traits his mobility and self-consciousness, and the former is emphasized in *Don Juan.* Adeline is so graceful a social performer that Juan begins to feel some doubt as to how much of her is *real:*

> So well she acted all and every part
>   By turns—with that vivacious versatility,
> Which many people take for want of heart.
>   They err—'tis merely what is call'd mobility,
> A thing of temperament and not of art,
>   Though seeming so, from its supposed facility;
> And false—though true; for surely they're sincerest
> Who are strongly acted on by what is nearest.

This is Byron's own defense against our charge that he postures, our feeling doubts as to how much of *him* is real. An abyss lies beneath mobility, but Adeline and Byron alike are too nimble to fall into it, and their deftness is more than rhetorical. The world of *Don Juan,* Byron's world, demands mobility; there is indeed no other way to meet it. Byron defines mobility in a note that has a wry quality, too sophisticated to acknowledge the tragic dimension being suggested: "It may be defined as an excessive susceptibility of immediate impressions—at the same time without *losing* the past: and is, though sometimes apparently useful to the possessor, a most painful and unhappy attribute."

This is Byron's social version of the Romantic term "Imagination," for mobility also reveals itself "in the balance or reconciliation of opposite or discordant qualities: of sameness, with difference; the individual, with the representative; the sense of novelty and freshness, with old and familiar objects." The great Romantic contraries—emotion and order, judgment and enthusiasm, steady self-possession and profound or vehement feeling—all find their social balance in the quality of mobility. Viewed thus, Byron's achievement in *Don Juan* is to have suggested the pragmatic social realization of Romantic idealism in a mode of reasonableness that no other Romantic aspired to attain.

Byron lived in the world as no other Romantic attempted to live, except Shelley, and Shelley at the last despaired more fully. *Don Juan* is, to my taste, not a poem of the eminence of *Milton* and *Jerusalem,* of *The Prelude* or *Prometheus Unbound* or the two *Hyperions.* But it is not a poem of their kind, nor ought it to be judged against them. Shelley said of *Don Juan* that "every word of it is pregnant with immortality," and again: "Nothing has ever been written like it in English, nor, if I may venture to prophesy, will there be; without carrying upon it the mark of a secondary and borrowed light." Byron despaired of apocalypse, and yet could not be content with Man or nature as given. He wrote therefore with the strategy of meeting this life with awareness, humor, and an intensity of creative aspiration, flawed necessarily at its origins. Mobility is a curious and sophisticated ideal; it attempts to meet experience with experience's own ironies of apprehension. It may be that, as Byron's best critic says, *Don Juan* offers us "a sophistication which (in a highly debased form, to be sure) we have already too much of." We have, however, so little besides that a higher kind of sophistication can only improve us. Whatever its utility, *Don Juan* is exuberant enough to be beautiful in a Blakean sense, little as Blake himself would have cared for Byron's hard-won digressive balance.

"A Waste and Icy Clime"

George M. Ridenour

One of the principal obstacles to an appreciation of *Don Juan* on the part of many serious readers of poetry in our day has been what seems to them the irresponsible nature of Byron's satire. They feel that, clever as the poem undoubtedly is in parts, taken as a whole it is immature, exhibitionistic, lacking in integrity. This has caused distress on both moral and aesthetic grounds. But though it is not prudery to refuse assent to the implications of the poet's vision, it would be unjust to deny due praise to the style of that vision—its special grace and swagger. Certain obvious faults in the manner of the poem may be frankly conceded. Byron is sometimes careless, and there are times when he is obviously showing off. Sometimes, though rarely in *Don Juan,* he is guilty of bad taste.

But it is not these things, I suspect, that constitute the real problem. It has more to do with the uncertainty of the satirist's point of view as compared, say, with Horace or Pope. Satirists are normally conservatives and are proceeding at least ostensibly on the basis of a generally accepted (or in any case familiar) system of norms, principles, and attitudes. That this is not true of Byron in the way in which it is true of Horace or Pope (though the consistency of both is liable to some criticism) is clear enough. Byron is notoriously a rebel, and rebels have not enjoyed high critical esteem lately.

But Byron is not a consistent rebel. There is, for example, his apparently snobbish insistence on Juan's birth and breeding. And his views on women would hardly commend themselves to emancipated spirits.

From *The Style of Don Juan.* © 1960 by Yale University. Yale University Press, 1960.

But then what were Byron's views on women (or aristocrats)? They seem to undergo such remarkable shifts in the course of sixteen cantos that it is not easy to say. The apparent lack of structure in terms of which these shifting points of view can be assimilated is, I gather, the basic problem of *Don Juan* for the modern reader. It is not so much "What does he stand for?" (that is not always self-evident in the most traditional of satires), as "How do his various professions fit together?" In short, is *Don Juan* a chaos or a unity?

The question is natural and not unanswerable. The answer, however, cannot be in terms of a system. I have [elsewhere] pointed out that, even more than his Scriblerian predecessors, Byron had a temperamental aversion to system. He is not to be categorized either intellectually or poetically. But this is not to say that his vision is incoherent. It is, in fact, elaborately coherent. And it is with what seem to me the dominant modes of this coherence that I shall be largely concerned.

In the first place, Byron, rebel that he is, is perfectly willing to make use of traditional concepts for his own ends. Some elements of the Christian myth especially commended themselves to him both as man and as poet. Whether it was the result of the Calvinistic influences on Byron's Scottish childhood, whether it was temperamental, aesthetic, the product of his own experience, or any combination of these factors, Byron seems throughout his life to have had peculiar sympathy with the concept of natural depravity. Lovell has asserted that "Byron held consistently to a belief in the existence of sin and the humanistic ideal of virtue as self-discipline. The fall of man—however he resented the injustice of its consequences—is the all-shadowing fact for him." Whatever one may think of this as a biographical generalization, it is clearly true of the imagination of the poet of *Don Juan*—with the reservation that in the poem the Christian doctrine of the Fall is a *metaphor* which Byron uses to express his own vision. In *Childe Harold*, . . . he developed an original reading of the Prometheus myth for similar purposes.

The myth of the Fall, then, is an important means of organizing the apparently contradictory elements of *Don Juan*. In the context of Byron's reading of the myth, Helene Richter's and William J. Calvert's interpretation of Byron in terms of a classic-romantic paradox and Antonio Porta's very similar Rousseau-Voltaire split are seen as elements in a vision not readily to be categorized under any of these headings.

Byron introduces canto 4 with a stanza on the perils of poetry:

> Nothing so difficult as a beginning
> In poesy, unless perhaps the end;

For oftentimes when Pegasus seems winning
　　The race, he sprains a wing, and down we tend,
Like Lucifer when hurled from Heaven for sinning;
　　Our sin the same, and hard as his to mend,
Being Pride, which leads the mind to soar too far,
Till our own weakness shows us what we are.

(4.1)

What one immediately notices is the connection between this stanza
and the imagery of flight we have met with in the Dedication. One thinks
particularly of Blackbird Southey "overstraining" himself and "tumbling
downwards like the flying fish," or even more, perhaps, of the ominous
reference to the Tower of Babel. Here again a fall results from the attempt
at a flight beyond one's proper powers. And, indeed, the motif is recurrent throughout the poem. At the beginning of canto 11, for example,
Byron describes the "spirit," some of whose metaphysical flights he had
been discussing, as a liquor (a "draught," "Heaven's brandy") which is
a bit too heady for the "brain" (11.1). Metaphysical speculation is a kind
of drunkenness, and the image is one of genial diminution. Then, with
a characteristically Byronic modulation of the image of "indisposition,"
he adds:

For ever and anon comes Indigestion
　　(Not the most "dainty Ariel"), and perplexes
Our soarings with another kind of question.

(11.3)

Man's loftiest flights are subject to the unpredictable activities of the
digestive system. (The further modulation of the image in stanzas 5 and
6, by which physical ills, just now seen as hazards to spiritual flight,
become incentives to religious orthodoxy, strikes me as adroit.) The passage is only one of many emphasizing man's physical nature and the folly
of forgetting it or trying to pretend that it is other than it is.

But both the stanza on poets and the lines on metaphysics differ in
at least one important way from those passages in the Dedication which
also make use of the image of flight. In the Dedication, while the satire
is not merely personal, it does take the form of an attack on a real
individual or group. This is a common device of satire, and one which
Byron continues to use throughout the poem. But in *Don Juan* the satiric
implications of the image are characteristically generalized. It is "we"
who fall, and it is *"our* soarings" that are perplexed. Byron is making a

comment on human beings in general, on human nature. And if the comment is not remarkably optimistic, neither is it broodingly grim.

The point is of particular importance with regard to the first passage ("Nothing so difficult, etc."). For what Byron is speaking of here is not merely a quality of bad poets; it is something that he sees as characteristic of *all* poets, including himself. A poet, to earn the name, *must* sometimes soar. How seriously he takes this may be seen from one of his most extended (and savage) attacks on Wordsworth. As usual, in order to appreciate properly a particular passage of *Don Juan*, it is necessary to see how it fits its context. The passage in question, stanzas 98–100 of canto 3, stands as the climax of a variation on one of the most important themes of the poem, the social significance of language (cf. the Dedication). The section has been initiated with the song of the island laureate, "The Isles of Greece." Here poetry is fulfilling its proper function (as it does not, we are told, in the case of Laureate Southey), serving the real interests of society rather than merely flattering its rulers. For

> words are things, and a small drop of ink,
>   Falling like dew, upon a thought, produces
> That which makes thousands, perhaps millions, think.
>   (3.88)

Furthermore, in order to fulfill its social function poetry must be socially accessible. Hence the relevance of the attacks on Wordsworth's obscurity:

> He there [in the *Excursion*] builds up a formidable dyke
>   Between his own and others' intellect.
>   (3.95)

These, then, are the most important considerations lying behind the stanzas on Wordsworth with which the section concludes:

> We learn from Horace, "Homer sometimes sleeps;"
>   We feel without him,—Wordsworth sometimes wakes,—
> To show with what complacency he creeps
>   With his dear *"Waggoners,"* around his lakes.
> He wishes for "a boat" to sail the deeps—
>   Of Ocean?—No, of air; and then he makes
> Another outcry for "a little boat,"
> And drivels seas to set it well afloat.
>
> If he must fain sweep o'er the ethereal plain,
>   And Pegasus runs restive in his "Waggon,"

Could he not beg the loan of Charles's Wain?
  Or pray Medea for a single dragon?
Or if, too classic for his vulgar brain,
  He feared his neck to venture such a nag on,
And he must needs mount nearer to the moon,
Could not the blockhead ask for a balloon?

"Pedlars," and "Boats," and "Waggons!" Oh! ye shades
  Of Pope and Dryden, are we come to this?
That trash of such sort not alone evades
  Contempt, but from the bathos' vast abyss
Floats scumlike uppermost, and these Jack Cades
  Of sense and song above your graves may hiss—
The "little boatman" and his *Peter Bell*
Can sneer at him who drew "Achitophel!"

(3.98–100)

The first complaint made about Wordsworth is that he not only does not soar, he creeps. And he creeps around lakes, permitting Byron to emphasize his alleged provinciality and limitation by repeating the lake-ocean contrast of the Dedication. But this lake-ocean contrast is present only by implication in the explicit ocean-air contrast. While any flight is necessarily through the air, Byron is here taking advantage of its associations of triviality and bluff in order to discredit the flight of a poet whose characteristic motion is that of creeping around lakes. Byron's playing with the common Scriblerian notion of the proximity of the high and the low is brought out even more clearly by the highly Swiftian comments on the scum floating to the top "from the bathos' vast abyss."

But the satirist is also offended at the vehicle chosen for the poet's flight—"a little boat." There is something essentially improper, apparently, in a poet's soaring off in a boat, especially a little one. Perhaps he feels the symbol too private (cf. the final contrast between the fanciful *Peter Bell* and the public, socially relevant "Achitophel"), or, perhaps merely childish. It is not, at any rate, a proper bardic conveyance. Real poets ride the winged horse Pegasus (a persistent image in *Don Juan,* and an important one). Wordsworth's choice of a little boat, the satirist suggests, is a tacit admission of poetic inadequacy. Pegasus is far too spirited a steed for him: "He feared his neck to venture such a nag on."

In contrast to the creeping and floating of Wordsworth, the satirist bends and soars. The first refers to the natural gesture of the truthful muse, who is scrupulous in following her sources:

> A brave Tartar Khan—
> Or "Sultan," as the author (to whose nod
> In prose I bend my humble verse) doth call
> This chieftain—somehow would not yield at all.
>
> (8.104)

And this is by no means the only time that we shall be reminded of the famous couplet from the "Epistle to Dr. Arbuthnot":

> That not in Fancy's Maze he wander'd long,
> But stoop'd to Truth, and moraliz'd his song.
>
> (340–41)

In contrast both with the creeping and floating Wordsworth and the bending of the satiric muse is the soaring poet of the beginning of canto 10:

> In the wind's eye I have sailed, and sail; but for
>   The stars, I own my telescope is dim;
> But at the least I have shunned the common shore,
>   And leaving land far out of sight, would skim
> The Ocean of Eternity: the roar
>   Of breakers has not daunted my slight, trim,
> But *still* sea-worthy skiff; and she may float
> Where ships have foundered, as doth many a boat.
>
> (10.4)

One notices first of all the elements common to this stanza and the section on Wordsworth. Here again there is flight described in terms of floating in a boat. But what were there images of contempt are here images expressive of a disarming modesty (an old rhetorical shift particularly valuable to the satirist, whose pose inevitably implies pretensions of personal merit). To be sure, he presents himself as an explorer of the Ocean (cf. the ocean-lake contrast) of Eternity, but then he owns that he has no very clear view of the stars, and that his "slight, trim, / But *still* sea-worthy skiff" merely "skims" the ocean, floating on its surface. It is important to notice that while he makes no very extravagant claims as to his discoveries on the "Ocean of Eternity," he does claim some credit for having undertaken the voyage. He even asserts that it is of social (or generally human) utility, a point to which we shall return.

We are now perhaps in a position to profit from another look at the passage from which we set out:

> Nothing so difficult as a beginning
>   In poesy, unless perhaps the end;
> For oftentimes when Pegasus seems winning
>   The race, he sprains a wing, and down we tend,
> Like Lucifer, when hurled from Heaven for sinning;
>   Our sin the same, and hard as his to mend,
> Being Pride, which leads the mind to soar too far,
> Till our own weakness shows us what we are.
>
> (4.1)

The passage is, as I shall try to show, a particularly clear statement of one version of the poem's central paradox. For the moment it is enough to see how Byron is complicating the traditional images of flight and fall. It is not merely that the satirist's attacks on particular kinds of poetry and particular literary figures are elements in a more general criticism of a particular state of society (as the island Laureate puts it: "The heroic lay is tuneless now— / The heroic bosom beats no more!"). But Byron has associated the poetic "flight" with diabolic pride, and he means it. Whatever may have been his own personal convictions regarding the myth of the war in heaven, it serves the poet as an indispensable metaphor for some concepts and attitudes which seem to have been very important to him and which are of central importance for a proper understanding of his greatest poem. The movement of the thought is roughly as follows: to be a poet is a fine and valuable thing; poets, to be worthy the name, must essay the grand manner (soar); but soaring is a manifestation of the prime sin. It is this kind of paradox that Byron's reading of the myth of the Fall is designed to sustain and justify.

Byron most commonly, however, plays with the notion of fall in terms of the Fall of Man:

> We have
> Souls to save, since Eve's slip and Adam's fall,
>   Which tumbled all mankind into the grave,
> Besides fish, beasts, and birds.
>
> (4.19)

We have here at the very least an admission of man's radical imperfection, presented in terms of the Christian myth. Eve slipped, Adam fell, and mankind became subject to death. And—this is very important—not mankind alone. "Fish, beasts, and birds" shared the curse of death placed on our First Parents. Nature, too, fell. We live in a fallen world.

This fact may help explain Byron's notoriously ambiguous attitude toward the arts of civilization. They are at one time emblems of man's degeneration from an original paradisal state; at another they embody high human values. We are told, for example, that Haidée

> was one
> Fit for the model of a statuary
>   (A race of mere impostors, when all's done—
> I've seen much finer women, ripe and real,
> Than all the nonsense of their stone ideal).
>
> (2.118)

And of the Sultana we learn that she was "so beautiful that Art could little mend her" (6.89). Here, of course, there is the implication that whatever might be true of Gulbeyaz, there are women whom art might conceivably improve. But then we are told, with reference to Juan's dress uniform at the court of Catherine the Great, that "Nature's self turns paler, / Seeing how Art can make her work more grand" (9.44). The statements, taken in themselves, are clearly contradictory. But again this is not indecision or confusion. Not only do both points of view have their validity, but Byron supplies us with a consistent metaphor in terms of which the fact may be contemplated. That basis is again the Christian myth of the Fall.

Four stanzas preceding the last passage quoted, Byron writes of the new Fall of Man that will occur when, according to Cuvier, the earth will next undergo one of its periodic convulsions and a new world is formed (Byron seems to think temptation integral to creation, and fall the inevitable consequence of temptation). He speaks with some compassion of

> these young people, just thrust out
> From some fresh Paradise, and set to plough,
> And dig, and sweat, and turn themselves about,
>   And plant, and reap, and spin, and grind, and sow,
> Till all the arts at length are brought about,
>   Especially of War and taxing.
>
> (9.40)

The development of the arts of civilization, of which the art of poetry is exemplary, is clearly a consequence of the Fall, part of the taint of Original Sin.

I have thus far been stressing the negative side of the paradox. It is time now to imitate the poet himself and shift the emphasis to the positive pole. This change in emphasis may conveniently be considered with regard to the four beautifully modulated octaves with which Byron opens canto 10. He is here making explicit the mythic presuppositions in terms of which he is proceeding:

> When Newton saw an apple fall, he found
>   In that slight startle from his contemplation—
> 'Tis *said* (for I'll not answer above ground
>   For any sage's creed or calculation)—
> A mode of proving that the Earth turned round
>   In a most natural whirl, called "gravitation;"
> And this is the sole mortal who could grapple,
> Since Adam—with a fall—or with an apple.
>
> Man fell with apples, and with apples rose,
>   If this be true; for we must deem the mode
> In which Sir Isaac Newton could disclose
>   Through the then unpaved stars the turnpike road,
> A thing to counterbalance human woes;
>   For ever since immortal man hath glowed
> With all kinds of mechanics, and full soon
> Steam-engines will conduct him to the moon.
>   (10.1–2)

The concluding couplet of the first octave suggests that ever since the Fall of Adam man has suffered from a lack, a something wanting or a something wrong, with which Newton was the first successfully to contend. The reference is, of course, to the traditional notion of aberrations entering into a perfect creation with the Fall of Man, the crown of creation. Man, who in his paradisal state had ruled all things, now becomes subject to the vicissitudes of a fallen natural order. Byron sees a symbol of this state of subjection in natural man's helplessness before the law of gravity. The idea of fall, then, which we have already examined in connection with the Scriblerian concept of bathos, is here given much greater range by being associated with the force which in the physics of Byron's day was regarded as the governing principle of the natural order. As Byron sees it, since the Fall men naturally fall (morally and physically). The imaginative concept is very close to Simone Weil's notion of sin: "When . . . a man turns away from God, he simply gives himself up to the law of gravity."

The second octave is most explicit: "Man fell with apples, and with apples rose." In a celebrated passage of his journal Baudelaire observes that true civilization "does not consist in gas or steam or turn-tables. It consists in the diminution of the traces of Original Sin." But while Byron would probably not argue with this definition of civilization, his own views are rather more catholic. In his eyes gas and steam and turn-tables are legitimate and even important means for "the diminution of the traces of Original Sin." They are civilization's way of contending with and rising above a fallen nature. Scientific advance of the kind represented by Newton is "A thing to counterbalance human woes." And while there is mild irony in the picture of immortal man glowing over his gadgets and his steam engine to the moon, Byron's awareness of absurdity is clearly a complicating rather than a negating element.

Yet Byron is not merely (or even principally) interested in scientific advance. The art he is most concerned with is, as we have seen, the art of poetry:

> And wherefore this exordium?—Why, just now,
> In taking up this paltry sheet of paper,
> My bosom underwent a glorious glow,
> And my internal spirit cut a caper:
> And though so much inferior, as I know,
> To those who, by the dint of glass and vapour,
> Discover stars, and sail in the wind's eye,
> I wish to do as much by Poesy.
>
> In the wind's eye I have sailed, and sail; but for
> The stars, I own my telescope is dim;
> But at the least I have shunned the common shore,
> And leaving land far out of sight, would skim
> The Ocean of Eternity: the roar
> Of breakers has not daunted my slight, trim,
> But *still* sea-worthy skiff; and she may float
> Where ships have foundered, as doth many a boat.
>
> (10.3–4)

We have met this last stanza before. Here the poet, who has been discussing scientific investigation, applies the image of exploration to his own pursuit. If Newton was an explorer, so too in his modest way is he. This is a corollary to what he has said about the necessity of poetic "flight," the social utility of poetry, and the importance of a poet's rising above provinciality. The poet, who has been speaking of how science helps repair the faults in nature that arose as a result of the Fall, announces that it is his aim "to do the same by Poesy." Poetry too, then, is being seen as not merely emotional relief (though it is that) or relief from ennui (though it is that too), but "A thing to counterbalance human woes," an agent of civilization in its struggle for "the diminution of the traces of Original Sin."

The point is made only slightly less explicitly in the first two stanzas of canto 7:

> O Love! O Glory! what are ye who fly
>   Around us ever, rarely to alight?
> There's not a meteor in the polar sky
>   Of such transcendent and more fleeting flight.
> Chill, and chained to cold earth, we lift on high
>   Our eyes in search of either lovely light;
> A thousand and a thousand colours they
> Assume, then leave us on our freezing way.
>
> And such as they are, such my present tale is,
>   A nondescript and ever-varying rhyme,
> A versified Aurora Borealis,
>   Which flashes o'er a waste and icy clime.
> When we know what all are, we must bewail us,
>   But ne'ertheless I hope it is no crime
> To laugh at *all* things—for I wish to know
> *What,* after *all,* are *all* things—but a *show?*
>
>   (7.1–2)

The claims here are rather more modest, but the principle is the same. Byron's "wasteland" symbol is that of a frozen world. Since Byron sometimes believed in Cuvier's theory of periodic destruction and re-creation of the earth, and since on at least one occasion he conceived the annihilation of life on our world as the result of freezing (in the fragment "Darkness"), he may be thinking of a kind of progressive chill leading to final annihilation. At any rate the "icy clime" is not a cultural wasteland. It is presented rather as a state natural to man, an inevitable symbol of a fallen world. Man is "chained to cold earth" (like Prometheus on "icy Caucasus") and is able to alleviate his sufferings only by his own efforts—by love and glory and, as we learn in the second stanza, by poetry. This very poem is presented as an attempt to give color, form, warmth to a world naturally colorless, indefinite, and chill.

The poem, like the meteor, exercises a double function. First of all, it sheds light ("flashes o'er a waste and icy clime"), the light that reveals the rather grim truth about the state of man on earth ("when we know what all are, we must bewail us"). But the poem, even while revealing the melancholy state of man, helps him to come to terms with it. The act of exposing the sad reality exposes the absurdity of the pretense that it is otherwise, while providing through art a means of dealing with it without the hypocrisy and self-deception integral to Love and Glory:

> Dogs, or men!—for I flatter you in saying
>   That ye are dogs—your betters far—ye may
> Read, or read not, what I am now essaying
>   To show ye what ye are in every way.
> As little as the moon stops for the baying
>   Of wolves, will the bright Muse withdraw one ray
> From out her skies—then howl your idle wrath!
> While she still silvers o'er your gloomy path.
>
> (7.7)

This I take to be the true rationale behind the alleged "cynicism" of *Don Juan*. It is thus a prime expression of the positive pole of the paradox whose negative aspects we have already examined.

Don Juan: Form

Jerome J. McGann

[There was a] remarkable pattern of apparent fortuitousness in Byron's life. He did not set out to be a poet, but it happened anyway; he did not mean to continue writing poetry, but he did anyway; he did not begin *Don Juan* with any plan to write an epic, but so it happened anyhow. Chance, or perhaps a Fate with which Byron secretly cooperated, seems to function in the smallest particulars of his life, and his verse everywhere smacks of the occasional. In any event, his own plans, such as they were, are perpetually thwarted or changed. *Hints from Horace* was what he wanted to publish in 1812, but *Childe Harold I–II* came out instead; and the latter was designed very differently, both in 1809 (when it was first begun) and in 1811 (when it was first completed) from what finally appeared in print in 1812.

The instances could be multiplied with ease. But Byron himself made the point unequivocally when he spoke, early and late and repeatedly, against the idea of planning anything. The usual attitude of poets—of Wordsworth, for example, of Tennyson, of Eliot—is that one sees the end in one's beginning. Poets reveal, it is said, the underlying law or pattern or harmony of life in the correspondent harmony of their poetry. Thus probability is understood to be necessary to plot because a probable plot exposes the law which governs all events. Similarly, epic poets continually begin *in medias res* because such a narrative procedure establishes the need for an explicatory context. The convention of *in medias res* puts

From *Don Juan in Context.* © 1976 by the University of Chicago. The University of Chicago Press, 1976.

the reader in suspense, not about what will happen, but about how and why the present state of affairs came to be. *In medias res* enforces the desire to understand events in terms of an orderliness that springs from causes and natural consequences. To begin *in medias res* is to ensure that the events of the epic will be set only in the context of what is relevant to them. It is a probability device.

Don Juan is different. It explicitly does not begin *in medias res* and its arrangement scarcely covets probability. So far from planning the course of events, Byron positively suggests that his own method of writing is as unplanned as Juan's foresight is limited: "the fact is that I have nothing planned" (4.5). Byron is so committed to the unplanned form that, in the midst of the English cantos, he even admits his own uncertainty about the outcome of the events:

> Above all, I beg all men to forebear
>   Anticipating aught about the matter:
> They'll only make mistakes about the fair,
>   And Juan too, especially the latter.
> And I shall take a much more serious air
>   Than I have yet done in this Epic Satire.
> It is not clear that Adeline and Juan
> Will fall; but if they do, 'twill be their ruin.
>
> (14.99)

This pattern of unforeseen consequences operates throughout *Don Juan*— "Few mortals know what end they would be at" (1.133)—and it is based upon Byron's assessment of his own life as well as the general idea that too many factors impinge upon an event for anyone to be able to know at the time what it means, or where it will lead. And after the event, in the apparent security of retrospective understanding, the chains of causation and relationship which one perceives represent themselves not as the operation of necessary order but as a bizarre series of coincidental linkages. The result of a Byronic narrative in *Don Juan* is not even retrospectively a sense of probabilities but of achieved possibilities. Not everything has been assimilated, and the narrative line, as a result, seems factive rather than fictive. Events might have been otherwise, and with just as much reason, but they weren't. The end of canto 1 as we know it differs markedly from the end of the canto as it was originally written, yet in regard to probabilities one could not possibly say that the one conclusion is more probable than the other. Both were possible; but only one was chosen, and though the reasons for the choice are good ones, they have nothing whatever to do with the criterion of probability.

Don Juan is a network of such patterns. Donna Inez and all the characters in the first episode have their own designs and purposes on the events, but nothing turns out as any of them had hoped or expected. In the second episode, Nature's large forces stand as the very symbol of the unforeseen factor in life. As far as Juan is concerned, that he is saved from death at sea, that he meets a lovely girl who instantly falls in love with him, and that Lambro eventually comes to break up his temporary bliss, are all fortuitous and improbable events. Furthermore, if Lambro is the unforeseen factor that will destroy Juan's good fortune, Juan is a completely improbable event in Lambro's life. Thus the work proceeds, until the English cantos, where Byron sets up such a complex set of interacting forces and characters that the fortuitous method of the poem reaches its very apotheosis. So when Byron says at the end of canto 14 that "it is not clear" how everything will turn out, he is speaking the literal truth, not only for this last episode, but for the poem as a whole.

The stories in *Don Juan* are, in short, surprising, both to the characters involved in them and to the reader who follows their courses. Furthermore, although Byron as narrator is generally presumed to know the outcome of his anecdotes in advance, he himself tells us that this need not be the case. The admission is highly significant for the entire poem since it underlines Byron's own continual sense of surprise in relation to what he is saying: "note or text, / I never know the word which will come next" (9.41). When he tells us, at various points, about his "plans" for the poem ("A panorama view of Hell's in training," (1.200), we are meant to take what he says seriously, but not definitively. He may change his mind, or may be forced to by immediate circumstances. This is why he says that he writes about "what may suit or may not suit my story" (15.9), and why he does not worry much about the outcome, for

> In play, there are two pleasures for your choosing,
> The one is winning—and the other losing.
>
> (14.12)

If we are unequal to the precision of Byron's language, the surface wit of these jokes may conceal the point of what he is saying and doing. The remarks locate Byron's sense that the true significance of sequential events is not that they confirm a wonderful, harmonious order in the world but that they reveal the equally wonderful, apparently endless, and yet finite possibilities of order and disorder. Something is indeed evermore about to be for Byron, but equally something is evermore about *not* to be.

Wordsworth echoes Milton, in the first book of *The Prelude,* when he asserts that "the road lies plain before me" (1.640): this is the confidence that all things will be cooperant to a mighty end. But in *Don Juan* Byron echoes the same passage from *Paradise Lost* differently: "The World is all before me—or behind" (14.9). The remark is not a simple joke but a profound appreciation of the fact that any immediate moment localizes orders that are equally lost and gained. Not every event is cooperant to a single end of harmony; some things are used, some are not, and in any event everything is used in more ways than anyone could ever imagine.

Such a view has often been called Byron's "nihilism." But the charge represents a reader's reaction, not a Byronic attitude.

> I perch upon an humbler promontory,
>   Amidst life's infinite variety:
> With no great care for what is nicknamed glory,
>   But speculating as I cast mine eye
> On what may suit or may not suit my story,
>   And never straining hard to versify,
> I rattle on exactly as I'd talk
> With any body in a ride or walk.
>
> (15.19)

Byron's sense of wonder is for the extent of the world's variety, which represents an "Order" beyond our desire or imaginings. In *Don Juan,* Byron makes a great virtue of not comprehending the world in a unified, integrative, or closed system. By giving in completely to the surprises of his life, by emphasizing that, even in retrospect, one appreciates and can respond to more than the achieved order of events, Byron in fact opens his mind not merely to further experiences as such, but to further, possibly altogether different, experiences of order. Byron's world is not a system; it is a network of systems and orders, some of which may overlap in some ways, some of which do not.

The Raucocanti interlude in canto 4 (79–117) illustrates these matters very well. Byron could have made much of this episode had he chosen to do so. His experiences at Drury Lane gave him plenty of factual material to deal with this set of characters in full narrative treatment. But the stanzas remain an interlude and impinge upon Juan's history only in the most tenuous way. The stanzas might have figured in the whole course of *Don Juan* differently (or not at all); nevertheless, they remain as they are. Raucocanti and his friends appear suddenly and suddenly drop away, like some ephemeral species in a Darwinian vision that came and went, serving a purpose which the poem comprehends but which it does not exhaust. The Raucocanti interlude means what it says, but part of what it says is that it might have meant more (or less) to Byron's poem.

The key to the form of *Don Juan,* then, is the episodic method, where fortuitousness, not probability, is sought, and where plans and designs operate only in restricted ways. The poem is larger than its running and changing designs. Byron himself does not control his poem preveniently, or even pretend to grasp everything he has to say: "I don't pretend that I quite understand / My own meaning when I would be *very* fine" (4.5). Like the "unriddled wonder / The world," *Don Juan* is a "grand poetic riddle" (8.139) for both Byron and his reader. The poem is punctuated with phrases like "God knows who," but it does not presume to understand what is suggested by the verbalization "God." Indeed, the idea of a Divine Plan is itself represented as one of man's hypotheses.

> If it be chance; or if it be according
>   To the Old Text, still better:—lest it should
> Turn out so, we'll say nothing 'gainst the wording,
>   As several people think such hazards rude.
> They're right; our days are too brief for affording
>   Space to dispute what *no one* ever could
> Decide, and *every body one day* will
> Know very clearly—or at least lie still.
>
> (11.4)

Matching the episodic narrative is Byron's digressive and impromptu narration. Writing what's uppermost and "without delay" emphasizes not only how deeply Byron is himself imbedded in the flux of his poem, it makes Byron himself the poem's most consistent exemplar of its pattern of shifting designs.

> Also observe, that like the great Lord Coke
>   (See Littleton) whene'er I have expressed
> Opinions two, which at first sight may look
>   Twin opposites, the second is the best.
> Perhaps I have a third too in a nook.
>   Or none at all—which seems a sorry jest:

> But if a writer should be quite consistent,
> How could he possibly show things existent?
>
> If people contradict themselves, can I
>   Help contradicting them and every body,
> Even my veracious self?—But that's a lie:
>   I never did so, never will—how should I?
>   (15.87–88)

Such passages—they are legion—show what digression means for Byron in terms of the larger narrative context. The line of syntax forces us to receive Byron's ideas as if they were shifting reflections, as if he were revising his ideas as he went along. Yet this impression is only partly true. For if the line of verbal sequence frequently provokes further revisions of thought, the point is that all of Byron's "contradicting" ideas actually jostle together side by side, "in a nook" somewhere in Byron's "veracious self." The "surprising" appearance of such clashing reflections and revisionary ideas is just the sign that they are always available, and hence always present, in several senses. When Byron "contradicts" himself, he is not changing his mind but revealing its ability to see an idea or event in several different ways at nearly the same time. This is partly what Byron means when he says that he is "Changeable too—yet somehow 'Idem semper'" (17.11).

In such mental habits Byron presents himself as a type of the human being. Nearly all his characters exhibit a similar complexity of thought or response at some time. Indeed, the story forces its characters to reveal the "inconstancy" of their attitudes and so continually forces them to reveal a clearer image of what makes them human. Julia and Juan's "intentions" toward each other are a mixture of contradictory impulses and feelings both before and after their "fatal day." But the specific condition of these ambivalences shifts with the circumstances. Furthermore, when a character like Don Alfonso enters their orbit, as in the great bedroom sequence, the addition alters the entire gravitational field radically. Julia, in these circumstances, reveals a whole side of her character we could hardly have imagined to exist. Like Byron, she is a mass of contradictions and of course a very epitome of "inconstancy." But even her inconstancy is inconstant: inconstant as a wife and to her husband, she is a very rock of fidelity to Juan.

Don Juan reduplicates these complexities for reader and character alike. As the man both in and out of his own narrative, Byron equally undergoes and observes such experiences. All his digressions, from the most brief to the most extensive, illustrate this most important fact about the poem—for example, in the digression on "inconstancy" itself.

> I hate inconstancy—I loathe, detest,
>> Abhor, condemn, abjure the mortal made
> Of such quicksilver clay that in his breast
>> No permanent foundation can be laid;
> Love, constant love, has been my constant guest,
>> And yet last night, being at a masquerade,
> I saw the prettiest creature, fresh from Milan,
> Which gave me some sensations like a villain.
>
> But soon Philosophy came to my aid,
>> And whisper'd "think of every sacred tie!"
> "I will, my dear Philosophy!" I said,
>> "But then her teeth, and then, Oh heaven! her eye!
> I'll just inquire if she be wife or maid,
>> Or neither—out of curiosity."
> "Stop!" cried Philosophy, with air so Grecian
> (Though she was masqued then as a fair Venetian).
>
> "Stop!" so I stopp'd.

(2.209–11)

The simplest fact about this brilliant sequence is that Byron changes his mind in the course of it: inconstancy is deplorable, "And yet." He is moved to this shift, initially, by forcing himself to respond, as it were, to the delicate ambiguities of stanza 209.5: "Love, constant love, has been my constant guest." In stanza 210 he then seems to be wrestling "philo-sophically" with his inconstancy, as indeed he is. But the struggle, we suddenly discover in the end of the stanza, is not a simple one between a willing spirit and the weak flesh, for "Philosophy" is not all that it appears at first to be. In the end, Byron seems to have "stopped" with "Philosophy," and the ambivalence of that decision is emphasized in the succeeding stanzas, where Byron settles down to some penetrating "philosophical" reflections. Byron has his Philosophy both ways, as a "fair Venetian" and as some sage ideas as well.

To structure *Don Juan* episodically is to ensure that a whole will not emerge from any of the parts, and the digressions reemphasize this ser-iatim structure. To read this famous digression on inconstancy is not merely to observe Byron's own shiftiness. The passage explains why inconstancy is a constant fact of life by emphasizing the importance of context upon ideas and actions. Byron "hates" inconstancy because he (rightly) finds something incongruous in Juan's forgetful behavior. But he says "hates," which is slyly hyperbolic, because he knows that the reader will place these reflections in the total context of *Don Juan,* with all its extreme digressions. The word "hate" is exact, a sign that Byron shares our amusement at himself, and an invitation for us to share that amusement. Then there is "loathe—detest—abjure," a continuation of the hyperbolic "hate." The statements are, in one sense, unnecessary, excessive. But they work as amusement, at first, because they tell us that Byron enjoys our sense of enjoyment, even if he is partly the object of our amusement. The very next line, however, opens up a whole new way of seeing those first four lines: "Love, constant love, has been my constant guest." The line introduces a potentially serious, pathetic view of the transitoriness of love, and once again it is context which allows such an idea to emerge. For Juan's story is deeply involved, not only with many loves gained, but with many lost loves as well, and thus far the loss and gain, pleasure and grief, are pretty evenly divided. The other context invoked here is Byron's own life in love, which was then, and still is, mythical, and explicitly made a part of *Don Juan.* The myth is at once ludicrous and pathetic.

An explication of the passage in this fashion could continue, and in reading *Don Juan* these sorts of veering responses are in fact what we register. The crucial general point to be seen is that the responses remain seriatim, and do not accumulate to some more comprehensive or formulative intuition. This happens because every idea or event in the poem is continually being observed in contexts which shift our point of view on the idea or event. The basis of the joke about "Philosophy" in stanza 210 is simply that one is made to consider the term in different contexts— first against a conceptual background, and second within the highly concrete framework of a masked ball. We are thus led to see that ideas and events have their meanings determined only in particular circumstances and that the possible circumstances, or contexts of meaning, are highly variable. In the greatest passages of the poem, one has the impression that no amount of critical extrapolation could exhaust the meaning of the poetry—not because the meanings are mysterious (they are not), but because they are multiple. The result, as far as criticism is concerned, is that *Don Juan* encourages almost endless commentary but frustrates almost every sort of formal analysis.

II

This critical problem with *Don Juan* is directly related to Byron's polemical artistic purposes in his epic. Byron began *Don Juan,* as we have seen, as a critique of the most significant poetic movements of his time. Too often critics have read Byron's attacks upon Wordsworth and Southey, and the others, as mere personal invective, not to be seriously considered for intellectual content. I believe this attitude is badly mistaken, and that the vexed question about the form of *Don Juan* is closely related to Byron's critical ideas about contemporary poetry. Like his related *Vision of Judgment, Don Juan* is Byron's practical illustration of the sort of critical stance Romantic poetry ought to take toward itself.

Don Juan's digressions are the poem's plainest illustrations of its informality, just as they are the places where Byron most directly engages the argument about poetry with his contemporaries. Byron had heard Coleridge lecture on Shakespeare, he read the *Biographia,* he knew Wordsworth's "Prefaces," and he was familiar with Keats's early poetic manifesto "Sleep and Poetry," where Keats rashly attacked Byron's Augustan hero. He was, in short, thoroughly familiar with contemporary aesthetic theory, not only from his own reading, but from his frequent intercourse with persons like Hunt, Shelley, and Mme de Staël. Consequently, when he singled out the Lakers for attack, he was going to the fountainhead of the new poetic theories as they were being advanced in England.

Coleridge's ruling passion, as a philosopher and critic, was for the wholeness of things, and of the mind that deals with things. He himself called this his "leading idea." When Byron listened to Coleridge lecture on Shakespeare, he would have heard frequent references to this central Coleridgean preoccupation. In the lectures, Coleridge was careful to distingish mechanic from organic form:

> it is even this that constitutes . . . genius—the power of acting creatively under laws of its own origination. . . . The true ground of this mistake [of not realizing Shakespeare's genius] . . . lies in the confounding mechanical regularity with organic form. The form is mechanic when on any given material we impress a predetermined form. . . . The organic form, on the other hand, is innate; it shapes as it develops itself from within, and the fulness of its development is one and the same with the perfection of its outward form. Such is the life, such the form. Nature, the prime genial artist, inexhaustible in diverse powers, is equally inexhaustible in forms.

By the time he was ready to write *Don Juan,* Byron was seriously questioning the idea that creative artists can only work under laws of their own origination. Nevertheless, he would have agreed with a distinction which presumed the idea that particular forms were as various as Great Creating Nature. That form itself was important in poetry Byron of course, as a poet, knew perfectly well. He had translated Horace's *Ars poetica,* after all, where a strong plea for the importance of form is clearly, even initially, expressed. Nonetheless, it is highly significant that Byron should have chosen Horace as his arbiter of poetic form: the form of the *Ars poetica* has presented recurrent problems for centuries.

All of Coleridge's work reveals that, despite his insistence upon preserving the importance of multiplicity, his passion was toward unity and reconciliation, not only "the One Life within us and abroad," but the unifying principle of life in everything that is. In short, Coleridge is a determined essentialist. His remarks on "Method" in *The Friend* illustrate this passion to reveal the "Soul," the "Leading Idea," the "preconception" that subsists through phenomena.

> Method implies a *progressive transition.* . . . Thus we extol the
> Elements of Euclid, or Socrates' discourse with the slave in
> Menon, as methodical, a term which no one who holds himself
> bound to think or speak correctly, would apply to the alpha-
> betical order or arrangement of a common dictionary. But as,
> without continuous transition, there can be no Method, so
> without a pre-conception there can be no transition with con-
> tinuity.

These passages show that Coleridge's concept of form, while apparently quite comprehensive, is in fact self-limiting. For it is plain that an alphabetical arrangement could only be judged unmethodical by someone who had defined "form" and "method" in a certain way. Indeed, Coleridge's preconception is that a preconception of some sort must exist, both in Nature, and in the mind that meets nature; that *a priori* intuitions exist in the mind, and that there is a categorical imperative toward such intuitions.

Coleridge postulates exactly what *Don Juan* refuses to postulate. According to Coleridge, the purpose of a narrative is to convert a series into a whole. But Byron meant to sail directly into that wind, and to say, as it were: the purpose of this narrative is to convert the whole (i.e., the human world) into a series. Everything that is the case is taken for granted, not in the order of form, but in the form of experience.

Coleridge's idea about poetry is that it derives from the esemplastic powers of the Imagination, which were able to draw separate parts into a unity. The very word esemplastic is a coinage which he invented to translate the German aesthetic concept of *Ineinsbildung.* This theory, along with the formalist traditions to which it can reasonably appeal (both Aristotelian and Platonic), has dominated academic thought ever since, all but obliterating, in the process, the once equally powerful literary-critical tradition best known through Horace. Byron is a Romantic, but he is not a formalist. His tradition is definitely Horatian, that is to say, rhetorical and functional.

For Byron, form is not primarily something which one constructs to provide a poem or the world with unity; it is not even, in terms of the Romantic metaphor of organic form, something which one allows to evolve into a natural whole which is presumed to be implicit in the process of creation itself. Both of these ideas about form tend to see the poem as a self-generating system. In the *Ars poetica,* on the other hand, when Horace insists that poems be unified, his context for the ideas "simplex . . . et unum" is dominantly rhetorical and pragmatic. The poem's use comprehends an idea of form which is larger than, more important than, the simpler concept of purely internal poetic congruence. For Horace— and Byron definitely shares this view—form in art is function, or the use to which the poem is meant to be put. The poet "arranges" the elements of his poem not on the aesthetic principles of "the poem itself," but on the rhetorical principles of the poem in its relations with men and affairs outside itself. Consequently form, in the modern "formalist" sense, is to Byron only a part of the poetic product; indeed, it is the exact opposite of what we often assume it to be, i.e., the whole which is greater than the sum of its parts.

We see Byron's attitude toward form most plainly in the episodic narrative. Aesthetic form in *Don Juan* always operates only in local circumstances, and even in such cases form is severely restricted not only by the digressive elements but by the recurrent "improbabilities" in the narrative lines themselves. In *Don Juan* we have, successively, a series of episodes, and each of these has, in its turn, more local episodes still. But what the poem does not have is a supervening aesthetic form.

The reason it lacks "total form" is equally plain if we consider the very concept of form from a functional perspective. Aesthetic form restricts the possible arrangements of the materials to the laws of internal coherence. The idea of poetic self-consistency closes the world either to the scope of the poem, or to the range of the poet's instilled imaginative conception. The latter is the Romantic's situation, where the world of which poetry speaks must shrink to the limits of the poet's imaginative perspective on his materials. Everything that is the case becomes, thereby, everything that one view or "idea" conceives to be the case.

Byron announces his position at the very outset of *Don Juan,* in the Dedication, where he explicitly attacks the "monotony and mannerism" of the admired poetry of his day. A crucial element of his attack is that the Lakers have attempted to establish the limits of the case of English poetry. Like Wordsworth with his "new system to perplex the sages," like Coleridge with his "Explanation" of "Metaphysics to the nation," Southey is "insolent" in the very "narrowness of his imperial notions":

> You, Bob! are rather insolent, you know,
>> At being disappointed in your wish
> To supersede all warblers here below,
>> And be the only Blackbird in the dish.
>>> (stanza 3)

These men are alike in their "still continued fusion / Of one another's minds." The case is larger than Coleridge's "Metaphysics" may imagine, is larger than metaphysics itself; there have been more "sages" than Wordsworth, and perhaps better systems even; and there is room, in any *case,* for more poets than these:

> The field is universal, and allows
>> Scope to all such as feel the inherent glow.
>>> (stanza 7)

In short:

> There is a narrowness in such a notion,
> Which makes me wish you'd change your lakes for ocean.
>>> (stanza 5)

The Dedication is as republican in its literary theory as it is in its politics, and sets forth one of *Don Juan*'s most important ideas: that the more one tries to "soar" beyond the actual variety and experience of the world into coherent mentalistic ranges, the lower one falls, the narrower and more restricted one becomes. Order and comprehensiveness are not inward but experiential categories. The appeal, as Byron says later in the first canto (1.202–3), is not to Imagination or "fable," but to "History, Tradition, and to Facts" (1.203).

Don Juan, in this respect, constitutes a vigorous attack upon the

Coleridgean, and generally Romantic, idea of the symbol as the mind's deepest form of insight:

> a symbol . . . is characterized by a translucence of the special in the individual, or of the general in the special, or of the universal in the general; above all by the translucence of the eternal through and in the temporal. It always partakes of the reality which it renders intelligible, and while it enunciates the whole, abides itself as a living part in that unity of which it is the representative.
>
> [S. T. Coleridge, *The Statesman's Manual*]

To know by symbols is to make up for what Wordsworth calls "the sad incompetence of human speech" (*The Prelude,* 4.592). Byron opposes a discourse ruled by symbols, which drive into silence and ecstatic revelation, with a discourse of "conversational facility" (15.20). The structure of *Don Juan* is based upon the structure of human talk, which is dialectical without being synthetic. The syntax of such talk enunciates neither silence nor unity but shifting patterns of conjunctions and overlapping sets of relations. As in a Coleridgean conversation poem, or as in *The Prelude,* ideas and perceptions in *Don Juan* generate other, further ideas and perceptions. But *Don Juan* differs from such works because its associational movement does not build up comprehensively (i.e., "organically"). *Don Juan* accumulates by arranging ideas and perceptions in different ways, yet all the different arrangements do not make up one aesthetic arrangement whose "point" is to give a sense or intuition of the whole. The point of *Don Juan's* "piecemeal" (*Childe Harold IV,* 157) method is to prolong the experience, and the activity, of learning in the human world.

In "Thirteen Ways of Looking at a Blackbird" Wallace Stevens offered the following as an image of conflicting aesthetic purposes and interests:

> I do not know which to prefer,
> The beauty of inflections
> Or the beauty of innuendoes,
> The blackbird whistling
> Or just after.

Whereas the Romantic symbolist tradition takes its stand for innuendoes, *Don Juan* sought to recover an attitude toward poetry that was being put in jeopardy by Romantic programs. *Don Juan's* conversational facility argues the beauty of inflections despite the beauty of innuendoes, whose attractions Byron himself knew very well from experience (see, for example, "She Walks in Beauty"). If there was a sad incompetence in human speech, Byron knew as well the incompetence and limitations of poetic silence.

To illustrate his argument for inflected poetry Byron wrote a poem which, from our point of view as inheritors of High Romantic and symbolist aesthetics, does not submit to the exegetical procedures we traditionally employ. The poem will allow us to formulate not an *idea* about itself but only ideas about what it is saying at any particular moment. *Don Juan* argues that while the world is the subject *of* our understanding, it is not subject *to* our understanding.

We can see this better, perhaps, if we turn once again to *Don Juan* itself for exemplary material. Consider, for example, the scene in canto 5 where Gulbeyaz tries to get Juan to make love to her. The Sultana makes a formidable assault upon Juan, but he is immovable, largely because her approach has been so imperious and blatant. Don Juan has been, after all, schooled in very different sorts of lovemaking with Julia and Haidée. So his resistance is, in one sense, completely understandable.

> "Thou ask'st, if I can love? be this the proof
>   How much I *have* loved—that I love not *thee*!
> In this vile garb, the distaff, web, and woof
>   Were fitter for me: Love is for the free!
> I am not dazzled by this splendid roof,
>   Whate'er thy power, and great it seems to be,
> Heads bow, knees bend, eyes watch around a throne,
> And hands obey—our hearts are still our own."
>
> (5.127)

The entire sequence exhibits a rich use of verbal and attitudinal clichés which could serve an extensive commentary. I want to concentrate only on one: "our hearts are still our own." The question is, what does this mean here? Plainly, the cliché means one thing to Juan and quite another to Byron, or to us. Gulbeyaz is the index of these divergent meanings, as we see at the beginning of the next stanza.

> This was a truth to us extremely trite,
>   Not so to her, who ne'er had heard such things;
> She deemed her least command must yield delight,
>   Earth being only made for queens and kings.
>
> (stanza 128)

Gulbeyaz "speaks a different language" from ordinary mortals, particularly ordinary western mortals whose heads are filled with the clichés of democracy. Yet her wonder focuses our own sense that the particular cliché here has been marvelously transformed in current application. Juan utters a cliché, and part of the joke is that he takes it seriously as a sort of proverb, whereas we, like Byron, understand the context of Juan's high-mindedness.

Nonetheless, Juan is not being represented here, in his words, as a fool. "Love is for the free," he says, and if his grand pose is partly ridiculous—particularly in the context of his past (and future) love affairs—it also proves the "truth" of the "trite" idea he utters. Once again, context shifts our focus on the cliché, for Juan is behaving in an extraordinarily daring fashion to speak in this way to an "embodied storm" like Gulbeyaz. To speak thus, in fact, is to illustrate that he is indeed "free" of the power of Gulbeyaz's world. But once again we must qualify, for Juan is a certain sort of person—a young, fairly volatile man with fairly undeveloped powers of comprehension—so his "freedom" of behavior is partly the result of his innocence (and ignorance). Johnson, in this situation, would have measured his position accurately, spoken more discreetly, and submitted to his fate (stoically, of course). Nonetheless, we are forced to qualify further still, because in *Don Juan* innocence is highly valued, particularly in relation to certain kinds of adult behavior. But the qualifying process continues again because, in relation to what Byron approves under the rubric "judgment," Juan's youthful innocence is uncritical folly.

Two points can be made at this juncture. First, the exegesis of the cliché, in the context of the dramatic scene, seems capable of indefinite extension. Not only is the cliché transformed into the very opposite of "a truth . . . extremely trite," the passage suggests generally that we reconsider again what we mean when we speak of a trite truth.

Second, the meanings of the cliché have multiplied because *Don Juan* has put it to use. The factor of context, which I have just described, is only a spatialized metaphor for what "use" expresses in a more dynamic frame of reference. The various ways in which we understand "Love is for the free" or "our hearts are still our own" depend upon the interacting uses which Juan, Gulbeyaz, Byron, and, finally, we ourselves make of them. In the end, the method of the passage so dramatically raises up the importance of context and use that these ideas emerge as the ground subject of the examination. All of *Don Juan* is concerned with the presentation, and the immediate critical re-presentation, of this subject. For

Byron, ideas do not determine behavior, but the other way around. This does not mean that "Virtue" or "Freedom" are meaningless concepts for Byron, but that the many meanings which they have are determined by their use, or the language in which they have been, and are still, expressed. He sees very clearly that religious, philosophical, and political conflicts arise because different parties occupy different positions in the world and hence speak different languages. They talk, as we say, past each other—like Juan and Gulbeyaz. This situation is what Byron wants his readers to understand, in order that they may be able to engage in their own linguistic and behavioral acts with as much clarity and forethought as possible. Without such intellectual clarity, one cannot even begin to speak of, much less act upon, what a moralist like Thoreau (for example) means by "living deliberately."

Don Juan, we know, laughs away the quest for the Truth, much as Cervantes laughed away the Chivalry of Spain; but *Don Juan* rigorously pursues its quest for the truth. Necessarily, the quest is carried out in terms of history, tradition, and facts because all ideas—even, and perhaps especially, ideas like "Virtue" and "Freedom"—have to be *done* both to *be* and to be *understood.* History, tradition, and facts are Byron's ground not because Byron is a materialist, but because, for him, use and act are logically, and humanly, prior to ideas. Matters are accomplished before they are understood, just as language is used before it is conceptualized. History, tradition, and facts are, in short, the forms of accomplishment.

To see the world in this "radically empirical" way is necessarily to insist that Truth, even while asserting its claim upon Universality, is in fact a multiplicity. The pursuit of Truth is only one of the ways men have pursued the truth.

The Byronic Hero as Little Boy

Peter J. Manning

No contemporary reader of the first canto of *Don Juan* alive to current gossip could have failed to notice that the ostensibly independent characters of the story all reveal Byron. Anonymous publication provided him the opportunity not to hide himself but rather to facilitate self-expression and to tease his audience. Byron is the narrator (by the end of the canto the few attempts to establish a persona distinct from himself are abandoned), the unhappily married Don José victimized by a blue-stocking wife, and also Juan, the sexually precocious youth under the care of a widowed mother. Only a critical method flexible enough to regard such divided self-presentation as a legitimate subject of inquiry will reach the center of *Don Juan*: a reader who excludes on principle Byron's tantalizing play with the demarcations between biographical revelation and fiction sacrifices the essential quality of the poem.

In a paper on developments in therapeutic technique entitled "Remembering, Repeating and Working-Through" Freud observes that some patients who have no conscious knowledge of their past nonetheless reveal it to the analyst:

> we may say that the patient does not *remember* anything of what he has forgotten and repressed, but *acts* it out. He reproduces it not as a memory but as an action; he *repeats* it, without, of course, knowing that he is repeating it.
>
> As long as the patient is in the treatment he cannot escape

From *Byron and His Fictions*. © 1978 by Wayne State University Press.

from this compulsion to repeat; and in the end we understand that this is his way of remembering.

We must be prepared to find, therefore, that the patient yields to the compulsion to repeat, which now replaces the impulsion to remember, not only in his personal attitude to his doctor but also in every other activity and relationship which may occupy his life at the time—if, for instance, he falls in love or undertakes a task or starts an enterprise during the treatment. The part played by resistance, too, is easily recognized. The greater the resistance, the more extensively will acting out (repetition) replace remembering.

In the light cast by Freud the relationship of Juan and the narrator can be approached. The anxieties Byron remembers and reflects upon in reviewing his life, Byron-as-Juan acts out, or, to phrase it differently, Byron remembers by letting Byron-as-Juan act out.

The central critical issue raised by Byron's repetitions here presents itself. To the degree that his plots return again and again to the same situation Byron appears trapped in a neurotic compulsion to act out without understanding his dilemma. This assessment is offset, however, by the increasing fullness of exploration made possible by the detachment he is generally able to maintain in *Don Juan*. The free play of the poem permits him to contemplate his anxieties and not merely remain subject to them. What Byron-as-narrator recollects from the past loses its forbiddingly determined shape when it is transferred to Juan, and as it unfolds with unrestricted potential moment by moment in his present it acquires lively immediacy. The reader participates in each new incarnation of the old predicament, and looks forward eagerly to future ones. Like Leporello's catalogue aria in *Don Giovanni,* Juan's serial reenactments present compulsive repetition as comic reaffirmation.

A comparison with Wordsworth is . . . instructive. Looking back on his childhood days in *The Prelude,* Wordsworth discovers that they are so far removed from his present state "that, musing on them, often do I seem / Two consciousnesses, conscious of myself / And of some other Being" (2.31–33). His poem is an attempt to bridge that discontinuity through memory: as the poem proceeds the adult Wordsworth constantly reinterprets the frightening moments of his childhood as the benevolent ministry of nature, "all gratulant if rightly understood" (14.387). By its conclusion Wordsworth has fabricated a connection that is satisfying to him. In the words of the "Ode: Intimations of Immortality," Wordsworth declares the "vanishings" and "misgivings" of the child to be "the master light of all our seeing," and the inchoate apprehensions "before which our mortal Nature / Did tremble like a guilty thing surprised" he represents as the indication of "high instincts." Both the Ode and *The Prelude* resolve the dismay they initially record by thus subsuming it within the "philosophic mind." *Don Juan* illustrates equally firmly an awareness that "the child is father of the man," but it gives full play to the negative aspects of that inheritance which Wordsworth is concerned to minimize. For Wordsworth the traumatic events of youth are hailed as "spots of time" that disclose a rich meaning to later contemplation: Byron enshrines his trauma in Juan, whose arrest is permanent. Byron's younger and older selves, his "two consciousnesses" of Juan and the narrator, are nominally discrete, so that childhood experience is denied the positive qualities Wordsworth ascribes to it, and the poem implies a view very different from Wordsworth's belief in the coherent growth of the personality. The narrator, a victim of indigestion and metaphysical doubt, enjoys no sense of a central self, and Juan enters wholly into each fresh experience because he has almost no memory, remaining so passive that he may scarcely be said to develop a character.

Byron's permanently divided consciousness yields no integrated self, but it offers enhanced dramatic possibilities. Wordsworth movingly confesses in *The Prelude* that the "hiding-places" of his power were gradually receding from him (12.277–86), and the loss is the corollary of his successful ordering of his past. As he translated bewilderment into reassurance he simultaneously diminished the intensity of the recollections from which his poetry sprang: the imperturbable solidity achieved after great struggle by the man Wordsworth, attested by all who knew him after the early years of the century, closed off the peculiar unease that has been the strength of the poet. The double mode of Byron's retrospection enables him to relate the conflicts of his past in their original clarity and vitality, thus avoiding the fate Wordsworth laments and that he too had risked in striving for the premature synthesis of the exalted lyric voice in cantos 3 and 4 of *Childe Harold*. The perspective gained by locating his anxieties in Juan let Byron approach them as a joke and, thus defended, work them through rather than repress them. Juan's retreat from prominence before the ever more poised narrator of the astonishingly fertile last cantos is the sign of the genuine integration Byron's initial presentation of himself as split had helped him to achieve. It must be observed, nonetheless, that Byron exists in the poem as the continually shifting web of relations between Juan and the narrator. Should the two ever have wholly converged, or should Byron ever have identified with either alone, the poem would have stopped: Juan without the narrator is fixed, the narrator without Juan is a shell (hence it is appropriate that he not carry Byron's own name).

Manfred and the later cantos of Childe Harold suffer because their personal material is undigested: in effect they are insufficiently autobiographical and hence imperfectly fictional. In the first canto of Don Juan, by contrast, Byron depicts the formative events of his life, his experiences as son and husband, but so thoroughly rearranged as to raise a private past into a public fiction. The impulses behind the rearrangement are the key to the poem, for in retelling in this oblique fashion the circumstances of his childhood and marriage Byron is able to construct an ideal version of them, one that is favorable to the ego whose fragility is betrayed by the divided self-presentation. His spoof of the shorthand accounts of Alfonso's suit for divorce (1.189) undercuts the pretension to truth of nominally factual reporting, and thus slyly insinuates the equal veracity of his mode. He confronts the traumas that obsess him, but at a safe remove: what Byron-as-Juan painfully endures, Byron-as-narrator rises above, turning to comedy the bitterest elements of his own life and indeed narrating them as if they were not part of his life at all. The narrator, above the action and exercising supreme control over it, is an image of Byron as he would like to be, a self-reassuring demonstration that he was master of the problems that tormented him. The opening canto of Don Juan is the work of a man still possessed by the resentments that have obscurely governed his life, but it should be understood as an effort to exorcise them through the magic gesture of art: to neutralize them by exploring their causes, expressing them fully, and then converting them to fiction.

Previous treatments of the Don Juan materials present from the outset the fully-formed libertine associated with the legend. By showing Juan in his childhood Byron demythologizes the story and gives instead a psychological sketch of the effects of environment on character. The tale is less a chronicle of Juan's actions than of his education, and it is scarcely an exaggeration to say that Juan's education is his experience with women. His early life is dominated by his mother, Inez, whom Byron modelled principally on his wife: the allusions to Inez's mathematical bent and to Samuel Romilly, who had acted for Lady Byron in the separation, are there to be acknowledged (1.12–15). Byron drew on his own marriage in painting the quarrels between Inez and Don José, and details like Inez's spiteful attempt "to prove her loving lord was *mad*" as Lady Byron had done, make the parallel explicit (1.27). In this scheme Byron figures as Don José, but the reader recognizes at the same time that Juan is placed by José's death in a situation identical with Byron's first years: Juan left with Inez recapitulates Byron brought up by his mother. The compound of his wife and mother in Inez is profoundly significant. The presentation of himself as simultaneously the son and husband of this woman suggests that at some not wholly conscious level Byron descried at last the shadowy motives underlying the extraordinary behavior he exhibited during this marriage and the anguish of the sepa-ration. He seems in his analytical division of himself to intuit that the crisis of his relationship with Annabella grew out of much earlier psychic conflicts with his mother, and thus brings to the surface the true nature of the dilemma at which in 1816–1817 *Manfred* had only hinted.

The deliberately emasculated education to which Inez subjects her son exposes her sexual hypocrisy, but Byron also intimates the deeper strands of her character that generate it. Although Inez is not a sympa-thetic figure, it may be wondered how much of her fanatic prudery is the natural reaction of a neglected wife whose husband maintains two mistresses. The lack of affection in her life produces a corresponding concentration on Juan, as Mrs. Byron's did on young Byron. Her deter-mination to preserve his naiveté springs in part from fear that his nascent adolescent sexuality will lead him too away from her:

> Young Juan now was sixteen years of age,
> Tall, handsome, slender, but well knit: he seemed
> Active, though not so sprightly, as a page;
> And everybody but his mother deemed
> Him almost man; but she flew in a rage
> And bit her lips (for else she might have screamed)
> If any said so—for to be precocious
> Was in her eyes a thing most atrocious.
>
> (1.54)

Inez's desire to have Juan taught all the skills of manhood while yet insisting that he remain a child points to a type-constellation larger than the personal satire of this canto: the overly protective mother and the son whom she will at all costs make "quite a paragon" (1.38) but keep utterly dependent on her.

It is inevitable that Juan should seek to establish his autonomy, and Inez's desire to manage him by suppressing his sexuality pits her against a force to which she herself is prey. In *Don Juan* sexual passion is "the controlless core of human hearts" (1.116), continually breaking through the tidy patterns our conscious, social selves impose on it, refusing to be stultified and reasserting its turbulent primacy. Through the narrator's ironic disclaimer the reader learns that Inez's kindness to Julia is a pretense aimed at quashing scandal:

> Some people whisper (but, no doubt, they lie,
> For Malice still imputes some private end)
> That Inez had, ere Don Alfonso's marriage,
> Forgot with him her very prudent carriage;
>
> And that still keeping up the old connection,
> Which Time had lately rendered much more chaste,
> She took his lady also in affection,
> And certainly this course was much the best.
>   (1.66–67)

When Inez's prudery collides with the resentment that she cannot admit at having been supplanted by a younger woman, the emotional power of the latter triumphs. She throws Juan and Julia together:

> Perhaps to finish Juan's education,
> Perhaps to open Don Alfonso's eyes,
> In case he thought his wife too great a prize.
>   (1.101)

The affair does "finish" Juan's education, but only in the sense that it terminates Inez's careful sheltering: in a perfect satiric example of the self-defeating nature of repression, she becomes the agent of the catastrophe she most wished to avert.

At the moment of the lovers' tryst the narrator comments that " 'T was surely very wrong in Juan's mother / To leave together this imprudent pair" (1.110). The remark emphasizes the paradox of Juan's position. On the one hand he frustrates his mother by his success with Julia and so gains a vengeful independence of her, but on the other he merely acts out one of her desires. The aside underscores for the reader the recognition that Juan's first sexual encounter, which should be his initiation into manhood, is only an extension of his mother's dominance. There is no evidence that Juan realizes how thoroughly he has been manipulated, but his failure to attain freedom sets forth the pattern the poem will repeat again and again.

Juan's independence is further limited by the evolution of Julia, who is unlike Byron's later women in that the more she talks the less complex she becomes. Her tirade upon the night of discovery is magnificently theatrical, but it is of a familiar type. Byron's tour de force consists in part of making acceptable the reduction of a three-dimensional personage to a stock *intrigante*. The reduction is necessary if the narrative is to advance, since it would be too harsh to abandon a fully sympathetic character as callously as the poem drops Julia. The lovers are initially apprehended as equally young and innocent, but Byron continually suggests the extent of Julia's sophistication. When he retracts because it is "trite and stupid" (1.55) a simile declaring Julia's charms as natural to her as his bow to Cupid he prepares further qualifications. The narrator retains sympathy for Julia by depicting her as the victim of her passions and incapable of preventing the hypocrisy she practices since "Passion most dissembles" (1.73), but the similes he employs implicate her in a world much more ambiguous than Juan's. Her effect on him is compared to the wiles of Armida, Tasso's wicked sorceress (1.71), and her bower is said to be as pretty "as e'er held houri in that heathenish heaven" described in Moore's erotic verse (1.103). Over their first embrace falls the light cast by the narrator's sardonic reflection that "a good deal" of love "may be bought for *fifty* Louis" (1.108). Though Julia feels no wrong when her "conscious heart" (1.106) glows in her cheek, the reader questions an innocence that has been likened to the complacency with which Christians burn heretics (1.83). After such broad hints that Julia's self-deception is either wilful or of a moral blindness that approaches culpability the reader should not be surprised by her marvelous but equivocal apotheosis at the end of the canto.

The revelation of Julia's character, her vain delight in her many admirers and the boast of an "old and deaf" confessor intended to prove her devotion but suggesting the opposite (1.147), shows Juan as still the pawn of an older woman. Despite Juan's sexual vitality the affair rather impairs than fosters his growth into independence. The narrator calls him a "poor little fellow" (1.86), and Julia's maid Antonia, "an adept" (1.140), wonders at her mistress's passion for "a child" with a "half-girlish face" (1.171–72). Juan remains passive, not speaking throughout the canto. In what is to become his characteristic situation, he is saved from discovery by the ingenuity of the two women, but their protection also stifles his freedom. When Alfonso enters the boudoir Juan is effectively absent from the scene, bundled up in the bed, "half-smothered" by the women who shield him (1.165), and then crammed in a closet.

If one postulates with Northrop Frye that the archetypal comic resolution displays the defeat of the blocking figures and the formation of a new society around the united lovers, then the ending of canto 1 is a mixed resolution. The blocking figure is defeated, insofar as Alfonso is "pommelled to his heart's desire" (1.184), and, like Inez, brings about his own downfall, the public confirmation of his cuckoldry. But it is equally true that the love of Juan and Julia is broken off, and that aspect bears examination. It is typical of Byron's poem that the husbands and fathers who interpose between Juan and his lovers, however much they may be characterized as fools, triumph over him. This pattern does more than emphasize Juan's unheroic weakness: it is congruent with the melo-dramatic and tragic works, . . . and it clarifies the nature of Byron's comedy. Juan's enforced departure from Spain appears comic less because it is an escape from Alfonso's persecution than because it is a welcome release from the constriction threatened by Julia. Juan's near-suffocation in the bedclothes symbolizes the dangers her attractiveness poses, and he must leave if he is to achieve the freedom to act for himself. Since Byron-as-Juan does not have the strength to emancipate himself, Byron-as-narrator intervenes, immuring Julia in a convent and thus keeping the poem comic.

The circumstances in which Byron places Juan permit an understanding of the causes of his subordination to women: Byron's reflection on his childhood shows not only a dominating mother but also a lack of any men who might provide models of adulthood. Juan's father is dead, and Alfonso is not only a fool but also a rival. The tutor Inez selects to guard Juan in his travels is, like all her education, unfit to conduct him to manhood. Pedrillo's academic knowledge is no aid in a shipwreck, and Juan must save the man who stands to him *in loco parentis*:

> Juan got into a long-boat, and there
> Contrived to help Pedrillo to a place;
> It seemed as if they had exchanged their care,
> For Juan wore the magisterial face
> Which courage gives, while poor Pedrillo's pair
> Of eyes were crying for their owner's case.
>
> (2.56)

Even Pedrillo's *Imitatio Christi,* his meek death to sustain his starving companions, instead brings agony to those who feast on his corpse, a further instance of Byron's hostility to the Christian myth of the sacrificed son. Pedrillo's passing marks the end of the outward constraints Inez exerts on Juan, but the pattern of maternal dominance is fixed.

Juan supersedes his tutor and arrives on Haidée's island tested like a hero and ready to begin anew. The narrator insinuates that Juan has gone beyond an unselfconscious innocence like Haidée's (2.172), but despite his greater experience the configuration of son and mother reasserts itself. Underneath its surface freedom *Don Juan* displays a determinist view of character: Pope's "ruling passion" is given a foundation in psychological development. The plenteous food, warmth, and affection that Haidée generously gives Juan make his stay in the cave a return to the all-nourishing womb, and Byron insists that this shelter is also a confinement. He conveys its double nature in a characteristically rapid series of incongruous similes:

> An infant when it gazes on a light,
> A child the moment when it drains the breast,
> A devotee when soars the Host in sight,
> An Arab with a stranger for a guest,
> A sailor when the prize has struck in fight,
> A miser filling his most hoarded chest,
> Feel rapture; but not such true joy are reaping
> As they who watch o'er what they love while sleeping.
> (1.196)

Haidée's love is a maternal tenderness for the "helpless" (2.197) dependent who reposes in her care, "hushed as the babe upon its mother's breast" (2.148). Juan's sleep is an infantile regression from his fortitude in the shipwreck, as moribund as the state from which Haidée revived him. "She, / Who watched him like a mother" (2.158), is from the outset associated with death; because she is so appealing the threat she represents is lethally tempting. Even as she resuscitates Juan her "small mouth / Seemed almost prying into his for breath" (2.113). She wraps his sleeping body against the cold

>   closer, lest the air, too raw
> Should reach his blood, then o'er him still as Death
> Bent, with hushed lips, that drank his scarce-drawn breath.
> (2.143)

Here enveloping protection becomes suffocation, and what were only undertones in Juan's affairs with Julia become prominent. The syndrome is familiar: no sooner does Byron endow a woman with extraordinary powers than she becomes a threat to the hero. Because Juan is so close to Byron, the rebound is particularly forceful, and the violent shifts in tone stigmatized by many critics in Byron's treatment of this episode mark the depth of his investments in it. Byron's initial description of Haidée is filled with menace:

> Her hair, I said, was auburn; but her eyes
> Were black as Death, their lashes the same hue,
> Of downcast length, in whose silk shadow lies
> Deepest attraction; for when to view
> Forth from its raven fringe the full glance flies,
> Ne'er with such force the swiftest arrow flew;
> 'T is as a snake late coiled, who pours his length,
> And hurls at once his venom and his strength.
>
> (2.117)

The serpent in Eden is internal: Haidée appears as death because Byron perceives the longings for retreat she embodies as inimical to the adult independence he also cherishes. Through Juan he elaborates a fantasy of recapturing lost childhood bliss, and in his capacity as the completely free storyteller he extricates him from its powerful spell with the return of Lambro.

Juan's stature on the island derives entirely from his position as Haidée's consort, and the spectacular court they hold in canto 3 is based on Lambro's accomplishments, not his own. The rumor of Lambro's death which precedes their celebration is perhaps the plainest instance of wish-fulfillment in Byron: his lovers can rejoice fully only when the intimidating father who opposes them has been miraculously removed. His repeated reminders that "they were children still, / And children still they should have been" (4.15) enforce the regressive quality of Juan's attachment to Haidée. The "one star sparkling . . . like an eye" (2.183) which oversees their kiss seems a figure of the poet himself, indulging from a safe distance in the union of son and mother he has depicted. His invocation of the Madonna in the Ave Maria stanzas accentuates the maternal quality (3.101–3). The idyll represents Byron's deepest yearnings, but his imagination of the scene immediately releases his darkest fears. Byron describes Haidée and Juan as "happy in the illicit / Indulgence of their innocent desires" (3.13), and the import of the paradox, which has seemed merely facile to some critics, is easily understood when it is seen in psychological rather than moral terms. Juan has in effect stolen Haidée from Lambro, and his temerity incurs the wrath Byron invariably associates with any attempt to challenge a father. The oral fears of being swallowed by the mother are succeeded by oedipal ones of being crushed by the father. Almost as if he felt the need for expiation, Byron has Lambro return to punish the lovers. Haidée's dream, in which Juan's face gradually metamorphoses into the presence of her father (3.31–35), renders explicit the rivalry of father and lover often met before in Byron, and the encounter of the two ends as always with the defeat of the son. Juan is entirely unable to maintain himself against paternal authority: despite Haidée's intercession he is disarmed and despatched to a slave ship in three stanzas.

Haidée would not have become pregnant in the conventional romance to which this episode is kin, and her pregnancy reveals her essentially maternal nature. Her death without giving birth, like her swallowing-up of Juan, emphasizes that the nurturing feminine qualities that make the island a paradise are also inhibiting. Byron exploits the pathos of the sudden interruption of the lovers' joy and of Haidée's death, but the termination is evidently necessary if Juan is to be propelled on further adventures. The exigencies of plot, however, are not the sole forces shaping Byron's authorial choices. It is a nice critical question whether the involvement in his story the narrator conveys is merely feigned by Byron in order to heighten the reader's response, or whether it is the sign of an unresolved tension in Byron himself. No absolute solution to the riddle is possible, but in the narrator's deliberate, ironic dismissal of Juan the strong identification that requires the rejection can be detected: "Here I must leave him, for I grow pathetic, / Moved by the Chinese nymph of tears, green tea!" (4.52). In the previous stanza the narrator has contrived to blame Juan's misfortunes on Haidée: "Wounded and chained, so that he cannot move, / And all because a lady fell in love" (4.51). This distortion, presenting Juan as the passive victim of the woman who loves him, is like that in *Mazeppa,* discussed [elsewhere]: it indicates once again the ambivalent consequences of Juan's absorption in Haidée, from which Byron as narrator both dissociates himself and rescues Byron-as-Juan. The uneasy attitude to women visible in these lines, springing from fear of maternal dominance, is responsible for the fate meted out to Haidée. Byron moves his hero as in the tales from the regressive fantasy dear to him to the world of men, but the rejection of the supportive, enclosing feminine environment is accompanied by nostalgia for the peace possible within it. Haidée's death is recorded in an elegiac stanza (4.71), but the narrator abruptly closes his lament and returns to Juan with an admission in which Byron himself seems to be heard:

> But let me change this theme, which grows too sad,
> And lay this sheet of sorrows on the shelf;

> *I don't much like describing people mad,*
> *For fear of seeming rather touched myself—*
> Besides, I've no more on this head to add;
> And as my Muse is a capricious elf,
> We'll put about, and try another tack
> With Juan, left half-killed some stanzas back.
> (4.74; italics added)

There is no equivalent series of engagements and emphatic disengagements in so brief a space in the later cantos of *Don Juan*: after this point pathos is replaced by more aggressive stances toward the reader, and the narrator's voice becomes increasingly steady as the poem proceeds.

In the first four cantos Byron rapidly and indirectly reconstructs major portions of his life and career. As already seen, Juan's experiences comment on both his childhood and his marriage, and Juan's expulsion from Spain parallels his own exile from England. Indeed, Juan's cry, "Farewell my Spain! a long farewell!,'' cut short by retching, stands in parodic relation to Byron's own voyages as described in cantos 1 and 3 of *Childe Harold,* especially "Childe Harold's Goodnight" in canto 1: "Adieu, adieu, my native shore." The vision of withdrawal to a maternal harmony that in the tales compensates for disasters in the world of men is developed in its purest form when Haidée's island succeeds Spain, and then abandoned again in her death and Juan's second sea journey. The cantos cannot be taken as literal autobiography, but their very departures from strict accuracy enlarge their interest from another perspective. They offer a revealing picture not of Byron's outer, but of his inner, life: his sense of himself and of his past in 1818–1819. Almost a year, however, elapsed between the composition of canto 4 and the start of canto 5, and when Byron resumed *Don Juan* in the autumn of 1820 his position had changed. The writing of canto 4 in November 1819 coincides with the arrival of Count Guiccioli in Venice, ending a six-week period in which Byron and Teresa had been alone together at La Mira and the Palazzo Mocenigo. After some terrible rows Byron saw his lover leave his house with her husband, a scene that suggestively resembles Juan's relinquishment of Haidée to Lambro. The narrator's sentiments that it is better for Juan and Haidée to be separated than to endure the diminution of their love in time no doubt echo the rationalization Byron put on his own sudden loss of Teresa, but the depression was too serious to avert. He had counselled acquiescence to the demands of propriety, in part because continuation of the affair would openly declare him a *cavalier servente* and he resisted the regular attachment it implied. His frequent mockery of the institution in *Beppo* and his letters shows his fear of seeing himself as the "supernumerary slave" of a woman. The alternative, however, was worse: to Hobhouse he confessed that he felt "so wretched and low— and lonely—that I will leave the country reluctantly indeed." A wry letter to Kinnaird testifies that the new disappointment in love was intensified by Byron's interpretation of it as a repetition of the hurt of his marriage: "the Country has become sad to me,—I feel alone in it—and as I left England on account of my own wife—I now quit Italy for the wife of another." The proposed voyage illustrates the same reaction of flight from his troubles that Byron had fallen back on in 1816, but it was not to happen for some years. For the moment he remained with Teresa: "I have not been able to find enough resolution to leave the country where you are, without seeing you at least once more:—perhaps it will depend on *you* whether I ever again shall leave you." Though his grumblings at *serventismo* persisted, when Byron returned to *Don Juan* a year later the liaison with Teresa was an established feature of his life. His choice of Teresa is perhaps the strongest confirmation of the applicability to Byron of Freud's remarks in "A Special Type of Choice of Object Made by Men." Byron was entranced by her combination of convent decorum and uninhibited sexuality, a paradox of Italian women which matched the bifurcation of his own maternally-centered views of female sexuality. In her tolerant and unwavering love he found the kind of affection he had always sought, and her marriage to the much older and saturnine Count Guiccioli added to her appeal. By taking Teresa from him Byron achieved his fantasies of rescue and triumph over another man.

In Byron's initial happiness with Teresa the disquiet of cantos 3 and 4 abated. An index of the altered mood is the figure of Johnson, the Englishman with whom Juan is bound in the Turkish slave market at the beginning of canto 5:

> "Pray, sir," said Juan, "if I may presume,
> What brought you here?"—"Oh! nothing very rare—
> Six Tartars and a drag-chain-"—"To this doom
> But what conducted, if the question's fair,
> Is that which I would learn."—"I served for some
> Months with the Russian army here and there;
> And taking lately, by Suwarrow's bidding,
> A town, was ta'en myself instead of Widdin."

> "Have you no friends?"—"I had—but, by God's blessing,
> Have not been troubled with them lately. Now
> I have answered all your questions without pressing,
> And you an equal courtesy should show."
> "Alas!" said Juan, "'t were a tale distressing,
> And long besides."—"Oh! if 't is really so,
> You're right on both accounts to hold your tongue;
> A sad tale saddens doubly when 't is long."
>
> (5.15–16)

The formality of Juan's address hints to the reader that Byron is parodying an epic *topos*. In an epic that began conventionally *in medias res*
Johnson's inquiry would furnish the opportunity for the usual retrospective account of the hero's adventures, but Byron's commencement
ab ovo has foreclosed that possibility, and Johnson's lack of concern with
what the reader already knows is the result. Moreover, a full response to
Johnson would ask of Juan a small-scaled spiritual autobiography that he
does not possess the self-awareness to compose, let alone make into the
inclusive and brilliant meditation the narrator has fashioned.

Johnson remains an apparent false start in the poem, but he is nonetheless significant in its thematic pattern. He is the first man Juan has
met who is neither a rival nor much older—he is thirty (5.10)—and he
is therefore a possible friend and model as well as father figure. Juan is
easily drawn into conversation by Johnson's hearty, open nature. His
cheerful account of his three wives and his unassuming stoicism coun-
teract Juan's despair. Though the narrator will endlessly question how
one knows the "right point of view," Johnson's commonsensical belief
that wisdom is gained only through adversity is a moral of the poem,
its secular equivalent to the theodicy of *Paradise Lost*:

> "All this is very fine, and may be true,"
> Said Juan; "but I really don't see how
> It betters present times with me or you."
> "No?" quoth the other; "yet you will allow
> By setting things in their right point of view,
> Knowledge, at least, is gained; for instance, now,
> We know what slavery is, and our disasters
> May teach us better to behave when masters."
>
> (5.23)

Heretofore, Juan has lived only in the present; in Johnson's measured resumé of his own disillusionments he witnesses a maturity that can come only by learning from the past. From Johnson's calm preparedness for whatever may come he might learn to look ahead, and to consider the future without anxiety. Johnson has the foresight to correct Juan's rash impulse to attack Baba and flee the harem in which they are imprisoned, observing what Juan has never considered, that they do not know the way out. After their escape Johnson continues as Juan's mentor, introducing him to Suwarrow and then to war itself, the test of his manhood against men as his sexual escapades are its test against women. During the siege of Ismail he exemplifies the balance of discretion and valor wanting in Juan, retreating in order to rally while Juan thoughtlessly advances, loses his way, and endangers his life under the sway of his thirst for glory (8.52). Even John Johnson's name—literally, John son of John—emphasizes his affinity with Juan: he is Juan as he might grow up to be. (The parallels are close and numerous: e.g., Juan is about to have his third affair, Johnson has had three wives.) At the same time, his perseverance, bravery, and ironic detachment make him the double of the narrator, his surrogate within the action. However, since Byron has replaced the conventional counterpointed pair of picaro and servant with the narrator and Juan, and his scheme depends on maintaining their separation, there is no place for such a mediating (and duplicating) figure. Johnson serves his function—about which more shortly—and disappears.

The presence of a worthy and encouraging male figure, contrasting sharply with the hostile men who usually confront Byron's heroes, offsets the humiliating emasculation visited upon Juan by the eunuch Baba, who overrides his protests and dresses him as a harem girl. The transformation marks the uncertainty of Juan's sexual identity, and represents the collapse of the masculine image Byron's heroes have struggled to preserve. In Byron's world sexual roles are not determined by genes alone, but by power: as Juan is helpless, he becomes a woman. Concurrently, the beautiful Gulbeyaz who has purchased him becomes masculine because of her position. She is described as "imperious" and self-willed (5.110–11), exactly like Napoleon or the heroes of Byron's tales. Like them, she commands love and treats its objects like slaves: that is, like women—hence Juanna.

The reversal of roles contributes to one of Byron's most subtly ironic visions of the Fall, the archetypal event. . . . Johnson jokingly urges Juanna to keep her chastity "though Eve herself once fell" (5.84), and it is Gulbeyaz who assumes the figure of Satan:

> Her form had all the softness of her sex,
> Her features all the sweetness of the Devil,
> When he put on the Cherub to perplex
> Eve.
>
> (5.109)

Disaffected by her peremptory manner, Juan refuses to succumb. Thus Juanna does not "fall," as did Julia and Haidée, but her resistance does not proceed from innocence or mortal rectitude. In a Benthamite age Byron's satire is a reminder that actions give no clue to motives; Juanna's chastity is fed by a pride more vainglorious than Eve's:

> he had made up his mind
> To be impaled, or quartered as a dish
> For dogs, or to be slain with pangs refined,
> Or thrown to lions, or made baits for fish,
> And thus heroically stood resigned,
> Rather than sin—except to his own wish.
>
> (5.141)

Gulbeyaz's tyranny over Juan is another image of the threatening woman; the closeness of the scene to Byron's own fears is betrayed by a feeling interjection of the narrator's: "She was a Sultan's bride (thank Heaven, not mine!)" (5.111). It is not surprising therefore that Juan relents as soon as Gulbeyaz restores the customary notions of masculine and feminine by beginning to weep. The episode comes to a brilliant conclusion with the simultaneous arrival of the Sultan, as if evoked by Gulbeyaz's vacating the male prerogative. Her authority is in fact only a reflection of his: his appearance forces both Gulbeyaz and Juan—whom he mistakes for a pretty girl, accentuating Juan's impotence (5.155)—into the role of women, and so the rendezvous remains unconsummated.

Juan's humbling transvesture is a start on the path to self-consciousness because it draws a distinction between external appearance and internal identity. His resistance to Gulbeyaz is the first instance in which he views himself from the outside and gropes to make a choice, however melodramatically. His increasing self-reliance is evident during the night he spends in the harem. Juan's affairs with Julia and Haidée show him passive, constricted, or in a deathlike sleep. He now becomes active, capitalizing on his feminine disguise to approach Dudù secretly and successfully. Her Rubensesque form, placid nature, and likeness to a "soft landscape of mild earth" (6.53) suggest once more a maternal Venus, but for the first time Juan displays the traditional masculine initiative. Though Juan wholly succeeds only in a situation in which there are no other men to hinder him, the reassertion of his sexuality demonstrates that masculinity can be as effectively maintained through wit and skill as through the limited conception of "sternness" to which the heroes of the tales are committed: Juan's clever manipulation of his circumstances is a sign of his creator's transferred identification, from the Titans to the adroit improvisor of *Don Juan*. Artifice converts Juan's anxiety-provoking reduction into a triumph, and so the specter of the Fall dissolves into a comic anecdote of sensual dream followed by earthy gratification, the only unambiguously joyful treatment of sex in the poem.

Juan's fitful progress toward autonomy is hastened by his experiences in battle, the quintessence of the violent conflicts inherent in the world of men. Byron permits Juan to act out the rescue fantasy already considered: Juan fights off two Cossacks who are about to kill a Turkish girl of ten, and while Johnson is concerned solely with plunder, he pauses to guarantee her safety (8.101). In this work where Byron-the-narrator exults in his control Byron-as-Juan obtains without difficulty the status that painfully eluded the heroes of Byron's less comically distanced writings: he surpasses his father figure. As if to confirm that his usefulness is at an end, Johnson vanishes from the poem and Juan himself assumes the role of father by adopting the orphaned Leila, in whom Medwin saw Byron's own daughter Allegra. In this incident the close alliance between the rescue fantasy and the motif of the redemptive daughter is clear. Juan's rise to eminence in the world of men taints him with its savagery, and naturally produces the complementary desire to return to the tranquil bliss the child knew with his mother. A clue to the underlying mother-son relationship expressed in inverted form in the relationship of Leila and Juan is the narrator's insistence on calling her an "infant," despite her age: the repeated usage emphasizes the need to exclude any trace of an unsettling sexuality from Juan's affection for her.

Juan's thoughtless courage in the siege is a dubious quality: it wins him a place in the world of men, but his glory is the kind the narrator denounces, and it does not alter the pattern of his dealings with women. After the battle cantos Juan never again encounters men threatening to him, but he is far from free of threatening women.

Juan's ambivalent changes are accelerated in St. Petersburg, whose sterile imitation of life Byron captures in a precise epithet, summing it up as a "pleasant capital of painted snows" (9.42). Its ruler, Catherine the Great, is psychologically the least interesting of Byron's women. He accords her little physical description and makes no attempt to individualize her: she is the mere emblem of appetite, the "grand Epitome" of lust and war (9.57). Perhaps it is because Byron could not risk an extended portrait of a sexually devouring woman that he does comparatively little with Catherine, despite his fascination. As early as canto 2, in the midst of the Haidée idyll, Byron had intimated the connection between sexual drives and violence by an offhand allusion to Pasiphae (2.155). Later he suggests that the siege of Ismail could have been prevented had the needs that provoked it been directly satisfied in a meeting between Catherine and the Sultan: "she to dismiss her guards and he his Harem, / And for their other matters, meet and share 'em" (6.95). The sublimation of sexual desires into aggression is neatly stressed when their looting exhausts the Russian soldiers too much to rape the expectant and disappointed Turkish matrons (8.128–32). The connection of lust and war thus displayed is elaborated in the court of Catherine. Her unbroken procession of gigantic and faceless lovers betrays the essential nature of appetite. Because lust recognizes nothing beyond its own compelling drives and obliterates all individual distinctions in seeking satisfaction it is directly related to the destructiveness of war. Anterior to this portrayal is a view of sexual and aggressive passions as equally inimical to the stability of the ego. Juan initially returns Catherine's lust with the undiscriminating sexual intensity of adolescence, as automatically as he had fought at Ismail:

> he was of that delighted age
> Which makes all female ages equal—when
> We don't much care with whom we may engage,
> As bold as Daniel in the lions' den,
> So that we can our native sun assuage,
> In the next ocean, which may flow just then—
> To make a *twilight* in, just as Sol's heat is
> Quenched in the lap of the salt sea, or Thetis.
> (9.69)

The allusive texture in which the *doubles-entendres* of this stanza are clothed is unusual in these cantos, where the language is generally coarse. The numerous genital puns are a gauge of the depersonalization.

The theme that passion is hostile to true human relationships, brought to the fore at St. Petersburg, runs throughout *Don Juan*. Its propositions are too rigidly antithetical to adjust to the complicated demands men and women make of each other. Haidée's lineage begins in

Fez, "Where all is Eden, or a wilderness" (4.54); Gulbeyaz creates either "A kingdom or confusion anywhere" (5.129). The women of *Don Juan* inherit the syntax that earlier had belonged to Byron's heroes, and the common trait is further evidence of Byron's equal wariness toward the imperatives of (masculine) ambition and (feminine) passion. Drives break down the sheltered area in which play is possible and a self can be freely constructed. The narrator, defending himself against charges of cynicism, proposes that the lesson of *Don Juan* is that it shows the unhappy consequence of the inability to temper desire:

> The Nightingale that sings with deep thorn,
> Which fable places in her breast of wail,
> Is lighter far of heart and voice than those
> Whose headlong passions form their proper woes.
>
> And that's the moral of this composition,
> If people would but see its real drift;—
>
> (6.87–88)

The parade of moderation is self-protective: while he sends Juan into the situations most problematical for him Byron-as-narrator counters their turmoil by striking an unflappable Horatian stance.

Juan's rise at court extends and darkens the qualities of his relationship to Gulbeyaz. He is bought by the Empress as he was bought by the Sultana, and this time he does not resist. Juan internalizes his slavery, acquiescing in his reduction to an exploitable commodity. The sexual roles are again reversed: with full complicity he becomes a prostitute selling himself to a wealthy protector, lapsing into a dependent position Byron bluntly characterized to Medwin as "man-mistress to Catherine the Great." The ambiguous but there muffled implications of the luxury Juan enjoys with Haidée come into relief. Juan is increasingly assimilated to a commercial society that substitutes cash for love. The narrator says that he grows "a little dissipated" (10.23) and falls into "self-love" (9.68), which is to say that he judges himself as others judge him and accepts as if true the high valuation he owes to chance. Catherine's gifts block his achievement of independent adulthood, and with fine irony Byron conjoins the two most threatening women in Juan's life thus far by having Inez write to praise Catherine's "*maternal* love" (10.32).

A yearning for innocence preserves Juan from entire subjection. "In Royalty's vast arms he sighed for Beauty," the narrator comments (10.37), but he can do nothing against Catherine, the archetype of the devouring mother whose fierce embrace unmans her son. He falls ill from her attentions and the doctors prescribe travel, but that familiar remedy is only a palliative. Juan leaves Spain to pursue his education less corrupt than the society he escapes; he leaves Russia for his health carrying his infection within. Circumstances force him to quit Julia and Haidée, but he leaves unencumbered, free to begin afresh; he leaves Catherine as her ambassador, to be fully accepted by the highest circles of England's crass society and to become the focus of its marriage-mart.

The uncompleted state of *Don Juan* makes speculation hazardous, but internal developments and Byron's comments to friends forecast Juan's involvement in a new scandal and consequent expulsion from England. Juan's experience would thus parallel Byron's in 1816 and return the poem to its starting point in the autobiographical materials contained in Juan's departure from Spain. The several evocative heroines of the final cantos are headed by Adeline Amundeville. Adeline's casuistry in regard to her feelings for Juan recalls Julia, but whereas Byron lessens Julia's complexity he endows Adeline with potential richness. The justly-praised champagne simile (13.37–38), ending with the comment that "your cold people are beyond all price, / When once you've broken their confounded ice," hints that Adeline's emotions may erupt through her impeccable exterior, prompting an ambiguous "fall" upwards into sincerity even as they undo her. The unexamined jealousies which, presuming on the objectivity of forty days' seniority, Adeline misrepresents to herself as "maternal fears / For a young gentleman's fit education" (14.52), imperil Juan's precarious autonomy in familiar fashion. Her dazzling performance at the electioneering dinner she hosts illustrates her deftness at maneuver and corroborates the narrator's warning that she will be "the fair most fatal Juan ever met" (13.12). Juan is encroached upon also by the exuberant Duchess of Fitz-Fulke. In a symmetrical reversal of Juan's transvesture in the harem Fitz-Fulke exploits the superstition of the Black Friar and dresses herself as a man to entangle Juan in an affair.

The incipient relationship between Juan and Aurora Raby seems unlikely to survive the assaults of two such aggressive women. A Catholic like Juan, Aurora is guarded by that difference from the artificiality of English society, as is Leila by her Moslem faith. "She looked as if she sat by Eden's door," the narrator says (15.45), and though he differentiates her from Haidée the likeness is apparent. Her purity renews in the increasingly jaded Juan "some feelings he had lately lost, / Or hardened" (16.107) and rouses him to activity. Once more the determinedly pregenital character of Juan's affections is noticed: Byron indicates more than

Adeline's cattiness when in a speech of hers he rhymes "Raby" to "baby" (15.49). This glimmer of a tender relationship is cut across by the Duchess's escapade. The metamorphosis of the chilling phantom of the Friar into gloriously voluptuous flesh is a measure of the life-enhancing energies of *Don Juan,* but also of the anxieties that recur in the plot. Juan's encounter with the Duchess leaves him "wan and worn" the next morning (17.14), as debilitated by her as by Catherine. The narrator's directing attention to Juan's "virgin face" (17.13) is no mere arch dig in the ribs: Juan's passivity may be a kind of innocence, but it is far more ominously the weakness of a man no more able to control his destiny than a child subject to his mother's whims.

The configuration taken by Juan's experiences from Inez to Fitz-Fulke is that of a passive boy and a domineering mother. That is perhaps no revelation, and it is equally a critical commonplace to talk of the sovereign authority the narrator of *Don Juan* wields over his creation. It has been less appreciated, however, that Byron's ostentatious display of authorial command is complementary to the particular stressful psychological materials of the story. Yet even the reader who accepts the contention that Juan's career repeatedly reenacts the domination of a son by his mother may be unconvinced that there are intimate links between his specific inadequacies and the Byron recognized in the narrator. Some observations in C. G. Jung's essay "Psychological Aspects of the Mother Archetype" may offer further persuasion:

> The effects of the mother-complex differ according to whether it appears in a son or a daughter. Typical effects on the son are homosexuality and Don Juanism, and sometimes also impotence. In homosexuality, the son's entire heterosexuality is tied to the mother in an unconscious form; in Don Juanism, he unconsciously seeks his mother in every woman he meets.

> Since a "mother-complex" is a concept borrowed from psychopathology, it is always associated with the idea of injury and illness. But if we take the concept out of its narrow psychopathological setting and give it a wider connotation, we can see that it has positive effects as well. Thus a man with a mother-complex may have a finely differentiated Eros instead of, or in addition to, homosexuality. . . . This gives him a great capacity for friendship, which often creates ties of astonishing tenderness between men and may even rescue friend-

ship between the sexes from the limbo of the impossible. He may have good taste and an aesthetic sense which are fostered by the presence of a feminine streak. Then he may be supremely gifted as a teacher because of his almost feminine insight and tact. He is likely to have a feeling for history, and to be conservative in the best sense and cherish the values of the past.

In the same way, what in its negative aspect is Don Juanism can appear positively as bold and resolute manliness; ambitious striving after the highest goals; opposition to all stupidity, narrow-mindedness, injustice, and laziness; willingness to make sacrifices for what is regarded as right, sometimes bordering on heroism; perseverance, inflexibility, and toughness of will; a curiosity that does not shrink even from the riddles of the universe; and finally, a revolutionary spirit which strives to put a new face upon the world.

Jung's categorizations of masculine and feminine may be challenged as unduly prejudicial without at all weakening the essay. Anyone familiar with Byron's life as recorded in Leslie Marchand's fine biography may easily adduce evidence to support the applicability of these remarks. They penetrate the anomalies and apparent contradictions Byron presents, and, more important, they point beyond biography to comprehension of the structure of *Don Juan*. It cannot be said, for example, that Juan seeks his mother in every woman he meets, even unconsciously: he is too much a pawn of the story, too lacking in purpose and volition, to attribute to him the motivation proper only to a three-dimensional character. The mother complex Jung describes, however, may seem by inference a probable hypothesis about Byron himself, and it undeniably suggests a common ground for the fixity of Juan and the audacity of the narrator.

In Byron's early tales ostensibly mimetic narrative repeatedly modulated into a prolonged gaze at an unchanging crisis. The two modes, sequential narrative and lyric plaint, were in continual conflict, with plot forever yielding to static monologue. What Wordsworth remarked of his own poems in the Preface to the *Lyrical Ballads* is equally germane to Byron's works: it is the feeling which gives importance to the situation, and not the situation to the feeling. In this regard the difficulties the narrator of *Don Juan* experiences in trying to tell his story are perfectly genuine, because Byron's commitment to action and narrative is offset by the contrary urge toward expression typified by Manfred's cry, "My pang shall find a voice." In *Don Juan* Byron solves, or at least suspends, the problem by centering his poem on the narrator. Juan's adventures provide movement while the narrator self-consciously makes the contemplative impulse which had obstructed narrative into his most fertile subject. Freud saw the oedipal triangle as momentous because it marks the child's entry into his society: in *Don Juan* the rhythm of Juan's falls and the narrator's rescues of him, the recurrent plot envisioned in everwidening, ever refined contexts, reveals the very kernel of Byron's conception of himself and his stance in the world.

Byron's *Don Juan:* The Obsession and Self-Discipline of Spontaneity

Michael G. Cooke

> *It is the weight of memory that gives depth to new impressions; this can be an oppressive weight, but it is also the weight that may enable us, as we crash helplessly through the mazes of our experience, to break through into clear moments and wider resolutions.*
>
> AUTHOR UNKNOWN

The play of argument in romantic poetry may be seen to work not only to the internal advantage of a given work, but also against alternative positions and presuppositions. It has a securing effect for the speaker, and has also the character of a duty to discern, in the welter of values and experience that we now commonly associate with romanticism, tenable relations and underlying cues. It is important to remember that the romantics, if not bound to a given order, were bent on ordering what was given. This is equally the burden of Coleridge's manifesto on imagination and of Blake's *Jerusalem* (where a veritable babel of argument among all the figures in the work is finally resolved into a common sense by the poet and the concept of forgiveness). A certain pressure toward formalization is perhaps endemic in the human mind, and Blake expresses it for the romantics: "I must create a System or be enslav'd by another Mans."

The resolute individualism of that protestation mollifies its own underlying rigidity; to whom, after all, will Los's "system" apply? But the romantic period affords plainer, less personal, less emotionally charged

From *Acts of Inclusion: Studies Bearing on an Elementary Theory of Romanticism.* © 1979 by Michael G. Cooke. Yale University Press, 1979. A shorter version of this essay appeared in *Studies in Romanticism* 14, no. 3 (Summer 1975).

formulations of system. In musing "On the Principles of Method" in *The Friend,* Coleridge favors the enunciation of laws of understanding as a means of "controlling" events and phenomena; and Hegel, alike in his *Philosophy of History* and his remarks on stoicism in *The Phenomenology of Mind,* suggests a grand indifference to action and effect, a clean transcendence of personality: an encompassing and ineluctable system of time (*The Philosophy*), or an individual's system of "self-consciousness" in time (*Phenomenology*), defeats the local experience of flux and indirection. Coleridge and Hegel evince a desire to predict the eventualities of the world, and to enjoy the omnipotent freedom of foreknowledge. Blake, on the contrary, seeks but to escape some other person's prediction; his "system" is *to be formulated,* as a sort of perpetually indefinite defensive maneuver.

It would not do to deny to Hegel and Coleridge at their most systematic the romantic cachet. But it would be well to recognize that in practice, in performance, Blake's position falls much closer to the norm, which indeed proves somewhat less insistent than Blake's and more inclined to defend by evasion and undermining than by equal and opposite action. The project of "creating a system" would be in this light premature, and perhaps a tinge presumptuous. Rather a candid quest for fullness of recognition would occur, and systems or constellations or consonances might, or might not, eventuate. Everything may be expected, but nothing summoned, and especially (*pace* Hegel and Coleridge) not the future. The attempt to summon the past in Goethe's *Faust* and Byron's *Manfred* and Shelley's *Prometheus Unbound* had yielded only illusion and pain. The assurance of willed repetition is denied. The inevitability of Faust's cry, "Stay, thou art so fair," has its counterpart in the inevitability of change. The quest for fullness of recognition may be associated with the form of the epic, and we may turn now to Byron's use of that form as another act of inclusion.

The Giaour, at just over 1300 short lines, and *Don Juan,* at something over sixteen long cantos, have one crucial structural feature in common: both are fragments. Once this is said, it becomes necessary to ask if they are, as fragments, similar in kind (the question of quality need not even arise). Does fragmentariness express the same boisterous self-aggrandizement in *Don Juan* as in *The Giaour,* the same difficulty with aesthetic and philosophical ordering, the same misgivings about the adequacy of what has been written and the same compensatory faith that bigger is truer, as well as better?

It would be plausible to say that Byron left *The Giaour* unfinished, whereas death left *Don Juan* unfinished. Of course Byron amused himself with the contemplation of 100 cantos of *Don Juan,* a number so magnificent as to leave scant time for Byron's daily business of war and love, which after all pursued him ardently as he them. On the face of it the poem may have been not only unfinished in fact, but in Byron's own conception of it unfinishable, inasmuch as he meant to discourse in it "De rebus cunctis et quibusdam aliis": on everything, and more besides. Such a conclusion, though, comes too easy. It is only justice to urge that Byron not be censured for eking out with fond and wilful tongue a potentially tedious tale. He certainly knew how to abandon an unprofitable venture, leaving the pretentious Polidori to complete *The Vampire.* And as for his going on with *Don Juan* to no known end, we have perhaps been remiss in not recognizing the warrant Byron obtained from his time.

The unfinishable poem stands as a signal romantic contribution to the form and vital entelechy of poetry itself; it expresses a resistance to predictability in poetry, which grows in new modes, and has many fulfillments. The root problem with the long poem in romanticism lay not in the collapse of sustaining philosophical structures, but in the fact that the long poem could not, in reality or in mortality, be made long enough. Which is to say, it could not be infinite.

A link between the fragmentary and the infinite attests itself in various ways in the romantic period. The sense of incompleteness as an emblem of infinity may be derived from Keats's "On Seeing the Elgin Marbles," which seems to make the combination of art's perfection and time's depredation—a fragment in short—the "shadow of a magnitude." But in fact romantic philosophy is explicit about the symbolic value of fragmentariness. Novalis espouses it as our only means of approaching infinitude, and Friedrich Schlegel, in his uncompromisingly named *Fragments,* comes out against the principle of formal conclusion to thought on the grounds that the vital fermentation of intellectual process can only be rendered inert by artificial checks.

This is, however, not a way of committing thought, or action, or for that matter literature, to randomness. With a subtle echo of Shakespeare's "There's method in his madness," Coleridge in "Essay IV" of *The Friend* ("On the Principles of Method") sums up the combination of the casual and the purposive in the "cultivated" use of fragments:

> The true cause of the impression [the man of superior mind
> makes] on us . . . is the unpremeditated and evidently habitual
> *arrangement* of his words, grounded on the habit of foreseeing,
> in each integral part, or (more plainly) in every sentence, the
> whole that he then intends to communicate. However irregular
> and desultory his talk, there is *method* in the fragments.

Coleridge emphasizes that "continuous transition" is basic to "method,"
and at the same time warns that its *abuse* "may degenerate into the gro-
tesque or the fantastical." In a sense, then, method becomes the effect of
poising mind and matter between a wild versatility and a rigid unre-
sponsive form. Coleridge as much as demonstrates this by requiring a
"preconception" for the proper pursuit of method while yet assigning it
to a spontaneous development of the ordering (as opposed to merely
orderly) intelligence.

Other romantic writers, too, exhibit an aversion to arbitrary surprise
or disconnection, on the one hand, and to an empty rigidity or overrepetition, on the other. The latter we readily recognize from Blake's
denunciation of Urizen, whose forte is the mathematics of petrifaction.
Less attention has been paid to Blake's own resistance to the opposite
extreme of too much spontaneity and disconnection. But it is there, and
important, for between the extremes we can appreciate Blake's demand
for a poising of the self between its self-insistent tendencies and the reconciliation of the carelessly arrogant tendencies of things in the world.

Blake's equal resistance to overrepetition and to disconnection doc-
uments itself in *The Mental Traveller.* Against overrepetition he writes:

> And if the Babe is born a Boy
> He's given to a Woman Old,
> Who nails him down upon a rock,
> Catches his shrieks in cups of gold.
>
> She binds iron thorns around his head,
> She pierces both his hands and feet.
> (ll. 8–14)

Here is a superfluity of rigidity and repetition, binding piled upon nail-
ing, Christ's suffering upon that of Prometheus. But Blake sees through
to the fact that this is the obverse of randomness and disconnection, which
he equally condemns. The Woman Old continues working on the Boy
Babe:

> She cuts his heart out at his side
> To make it feel both cold and heat.
> Her fingers number every Nerve
> Just as a miser counts his gold.
>
> (ll. 15–18)

The individual Babe is obviously essentially and ultimately less than the sum of his parts, if those parts are separated and numbered. He may be wealth ("gold") to her, but becomes nothing in himself.

This graphically demonstrates a romantic uneasiness with *mere* fragmentation. Actaeon could not be taken as the representative figure, or even Orpheus, because they are torn apart *and remain so*. Shelley reintegrates Orpheus into the romantic scheme by terming language "a *perpetual* Orphic song," thus overcoming the piecemeal temporal effect of the root story. No, fragmentation is problematical even at the level of synecdoche; when Coleridge complains in "Dejection: An Ode" that he is disoriented and dispirited because "that which [in his being] suits a part infects the whole," he is showing us that synecdoche—the part for the whole—both represents and represses what it stands for. It admits the existence of the rest, but by a coercive homogeneity denies the range and character and substance of what goes beyond it. At bottom, Blake's "The Tyger" works as a poem about the poignant insanity of a man who truly sees nothing but parts, whose vision is a fearfully unqualified and unrelieved synecdoche, affecting alike the Creator and the Tyger: hand, eye, wings, shoulder, feet, and smile are the parts for the Creator, and for the Tyger, sinews of the heart, brain, eyes. The fragment, in short, is not being held up for itself and in isolation, but as a signpost—so to speak, an index finger—bearing toward an ultimate whole.

It is wholly in keeping with this principle that we recognize an ambition of the infinite in the way the romantic poets handle the long poem. It is clear in Blake and Shelley that the long poem (taking *Prometheus Unbound* as a poem in dramatic guise) is meant to encompass infinity, and the form of the works images this fact. *Jerusalem* ends at the ninety-ninth plate, but it makes no bones about the fact that the ending is a poetic fiction and an authorial convenience. Enitharmon advises Los that the poet, Blake, is about to wind up the project they are living, and so the action, the poem, moves into a landing pattern. Accordingly, we have not so much a conclusion as a resolution of the poem, which might have flown on forever and which conceptually does fly on forever, since the human states or Zoas with which it deals are timeless. Much the same effect is achieved in *Prometheus Unbound,* where the sober, if not somber, injunction of Demogorgon to struggle against relapse suggests a perennial tension, if not an everlasting cycle.

The *Prelude* may also be instanced as a poem boasting a sense of resolution rather than a strict conclusion; the principles of "something evermore about to be" and the contention that "our home is with infinitude" both convey a reaching toward as governing the emergencies of the poem's action, and that action, though so lucid and so comprehensive in the Snowdon episode, still remains open and unpredictable. Assurance is given, reliably so, but how to live up to this assurance will have to be discovered. Just as in "Resolution and Independence," a given solution is perennially to be tested and challenged by some inevitable, though unnameable, emergency. *The Prelude* itself constitutes a resumption and a recognition of its own action, with every suggestion of an everlasting cycle, in Wordsworth's mind, analogous to the everlasting cycle set up between William and Dorothy at the end of "Tintern Abbey." More than this, the poem's beginning in discrete fragments and its gradual, as well as endlessly self-modifying, crystallization in Wordsworth's mind make it resemble *Don Juan* stage for stage.

In the case of *Don Juan,* then, it would seem timely to ask: is it in the singular romantic sense an infinite poem, or did it only stand in danger of growing physically interminable? First let me say there is in the abstract no reason why we should not greet an interminable poem with perfect equanimity: it is nothing to us if we choose to ignore it. But benign neglect did not seem a possibility with *Don Juan* in 1824 and is not now a century and a half later; the projected interminability of the poem accordingly threatens us, as an extension of the fact that the poem itself threatens us, at any length. I venture to say *Don Juan* threatens the reader as no comparable poem does—*Paradise Lost* and *Jerusalem* and *The Prelude* are actually consolatory efforts, and Swinburne's *Atalanta in Calydon* and Hardy's *The Dynasts* prove, though forbidding, less than inescapable in vision.

Given that it is too much and too good to ignore, what makes *Don Juan* a threatening poem? Certainly not its theme of liberty, a very shibboleth of British self-opinion. And not the sexuality of the poem, where it falls far short of Fielding or even in some respects Goldsmith and Gay. Nor should it have been the multifariousness of the poem; an episodic structure is characteristic of epic and picaresque forms, as well as traditional in the Don Juan stories, and Fielding and Sterne would both stand as precedents for a multifarious form; Sterne indeed amuses the reader with his projection of the *opus sine fine*:

> I am this month one whole year older than I was this time twelvemonth; and yet have got, as you perceive, almost into the middle of my fourth volume—and no farther than to my first day's life—'tis demonstrative that I have three hundred and sixty-four days more life to write just now, than when I first set out; so that instead of advancing, . . . on the contrary, I am just thrown so many volumes back. . . . It must follow, an' please your worships, that the more I write, the more I shall have to write—and consequently, the more your worships read, the more your worships will have to read.
>
> (*Tristram Shandy,* chapter 13)

And yet in a way all three factors—liberty, sexuality, and multifariousness—help to make *Don Juan* threatening because of the peculiar and unconventional use Byron makes of them. For *Don Juan* first of all confronts us with a state of dissolutions. Within a brisk four cantos it dissolves the premier genre of Western literature, the epic, with a few perversely dextrous, or perhaps I should say sinister, strokes: the opening phrase, "I want a hero," is a scandal to the tradition and a far cry from Wordsworth's anxious reverent pondering and Milton's "long choosing and beginning late"; and by the same token the insistence on beginning at the beginning and on proceeding without a Muse, that panacea against poetic disability, helps to destroy any sense of orientation or coherence in a story whose center, the hero, is already "wanting." Here is an epic, that noble and conventional form, in which anything can happen. The extent to which Byron undoes our expectations and threatens our assurance may be inferred from the fact that his greatest epic catalogue occurs in a private letter as a litany of his recent conquests, and his finest descent into the underworld occurs on the morning when he awoke and found himself in a crimson-curtained bed with Annabella Milbanke, and gave voice to the ungallant outcry "Good God, I am surely in Hell." Meanwhile, in his ongoing epic, he proceeds to dissolve our towering estimate of Plato ("Oh Plato! Plato! you have paved the way, / With your confounded fantasies, to more / Immoral conduct"), and to dissolve the marriage of Donna Julia and Don Alfonso, Juan's ties to his homeland, our faith in the covenant of the rainbow and in man's humanity to man, and one entire Aegean island:

> That isle is now all desolate and bare,
> Its dwelling down, its tenants pass'd away;
> None but her own [Haidée's] and father's grave is there,
> And nothing outward tells of human clay;
> Ye could not know where lies a thing so fair,
> No stone is there to show, no tongue to say
> What was; no dirge, except the hollow sea's,
> Mourns o'er the beauty of the Cyclades.
>
> (4.72)

And having as it were immersed us in the mourning of the sea, while disingenuously denying the existence of any elegy, he is off again ad lib: "But let me change this theme which grows too sad."

The fact is that, as much as Keats would oppose this, Byron is his consummate chameleon poet, changing themes and schemes quicker than the mind, let alone the eye, can follow. And this is what poses a threat. Byron strips us of all forms of assurance, from the generic to the linguistic to the religious, offering us in place of this slavery of custom a freedom of the moment that is inseparable from its perils. He, however, having voluntarily cast off form and custom, proceeds effortlessly on his way ("Carelessly I sing"); we struggle up behind. He keeps his footing wherever he goes, even into the pitfalls of skepticism; we do not and cannot. In short, *Don Juan* threatens us because it does not lend itself to plotting and bounding, and as we trail after it we experience not only the exhilaration of its freedom, but also the embarrassment of its unfamiliar power and ways. We might delight in its unplotted ease, indeed we do so, until there comes home to us a sense of its unboundedness. It is hard not to pull back at the intersection of spontaneity and infinity.

It has been observed that every risk entails an opportunity; no doubt every threat also disguises an invitation. It seems to me that *Don Juan* poses an invitation to explore the problem of spontaneity in romanticism; it is only the most vivid instance of a phenomenon we can recognize in poems as diverse as *The Prelude* and *The Fall of Hyperion,* namely, a structure of collision and surprise experienced by writer and reader alike. Such a structure exhibits the kind of development where a ride in a rowboat, an all-night party, reading a book by Cervantes, or climbing the Alps or Mount Snowdon will lead to effects entirely unforeseen and unforeseeable. Significantly, this structure affects both the speaker and the reader; the poet who, say, enjoys a draught of vintage, is as subject to collision, as taken by surprise as we. Perhaps Byron for his part displaces his surprise, but he does not dissimulate his vulnerability:

But let me change this theme which grows too sad,
And lay this sheet of sorrows on the shelf;
I don't much like describing people mad,
For fear of seeming rather touch'd myself.

(4.74)

Or again we have his avowal that, strive as he may to become a "Stoic, Sage," "The wind shifts, and [he flies] into a rage" (17.10).

On the strength of such indications let me suggest that spontaneity is not all freedom and arbitrary lines. At bottom, indeed, spontaneity and a fatalistic tendency or bent run together, as do spontaneity and sheer local reaction. The things we describe as spontaneous, as opposed to laborious, are the things that coincide with our preferences, which after all constitute limitations as much as strengths; what the Spaniards call a "querencia" nicely suggests the rigid and bovine quality of a preference. Furthermore, we need to recall that the art of improvisation, which Byron so admired, is a highly trained art, and that, within the realm of conventional literary expression, romance flourishes on the art of *divagation,* of taking off in unforeseen directions. Allowing for the charm of a variegated energy, then, we must note that incoherence is anathema to the human mind. Closely looked at, how spontaneous is spontaneity? It seems crucial to stress the peculiarly romantic practice of clinging to random incidents as though for dear life, and of finding in them a cumulative pattern of meaning and value. For this becomes the basis and the purpose of the long unfinished or, as we may say, the infinite poem in the romantic scheme: to go over, and over and over, some material that we cannot let go, and to go into, and ever further into, the possibilities of that material, which becomes at once obsession and careful choice, fixation and source of revelation. And one is struck to find the same determination to encompass all acts and states, along with the same inability to leave anything alone—in short the same willed and obsessive spontaneity—in Goethe's *Faust* and Rousseau's *Confessions.*

What I am proposing boils down to this: *Don Juan* builds itself on the pattern of repetition and reflection and variation, of subtle repetition and oblique reflection and intricate variation, of the simple single action of the initial Juan-Julia episode. This multiform episode becomes the poem's central figure, or at least configuration: *Don Juan* revolves around a complex of human behavior rather than an individual character, and the poem's beginning becomes at once perpetual and final—if we knew enough of the exfoliating form of this episode, we would have to go on no further. Of this, more anon. It is well here to recall the positive implications of the avowal "I want a hero," which advises us of a need and active desire, as well as a brute deficiency. In other words there is an affirmative thrust toward reconstitution underlying the overt dissolution of the hero in the poem. In this dispensation Juan must choose to be a hero, and of what stripe; he will not find hero status thrust upon him.

The factor of choice in *Don Juan* is easy to overlook, but it is pervasive and can readily be invoked to show the reflexive complexity of the poem's design. Let us first recall its pervasive presence; Juan must choose—that is, he cannot, if he is to survive, choose but choose—how to respond vis-à-vis Alfonso and Lambro; it is fight or die. I would refrain from praising him merely for fighting here, especially since he does not do it well, and that only for the simplest sort of survival. But his fighting seems to anticipate and to be consonant with two other choices Juan does *not* have to make, in the shipwreck and the harem episodes. The latter choices, not impetuous but deliberate, not convenient but contradictory to survival, seem to me to enunciate a standard and principle of human dignity that the hullaballoo with Alfonso and Lambro somewhat beclouds. To choose not to die drunk and not to eat human flesh as a means of staying alive, and to declare to the smitten and nervous Gulbeyaz, "love is for the free": these are not the marks of a sensual or indifferent nature. Not that Byron goes overboard and sacrifices Juan's human plausibility to the pieties of heroism; the lad does at last, and despite "some remorse," allow himself a paw of his father's spaniel, and does treat himself to an incipient dalliance with Dudú. In a sense Byron seems to say that Juan's heroism, if it is to come about, must come from a personal and moral act of his nature rather than from an aesthetic definition of character established by genre or authorial fiat. Thus the choices he continues to be faced with convey intuitions or intimations of deeper being; the act of saving Leila momentarily stems the tide of his commitment to the inhuman siege; the choice of becoming the Empress Catherine's plaything—a far cry from his defiance of the more sympathetic Gulbeyaz—proves a choice of spiritual and physical dissipation.

The final choice of the poem as we have it involves a recapitulation of the individual moments we have seen Juan in before: the bossy Lady Adeline Amundeville, the sensual Duchess of Fitz-Fulke, and the refined and lovely Aurora bring back Gulbeyaz-Catherine, Julia and Haidée respectively. Juan has a second chance, with the intensities and precipitancies of first experience now tempered by reflection and comparison, to choose what kind of man he will be, in terms of what kind of woman he will identify himself with. Such a choice has been adumbrated in the harem episode, where Lolah, Katinka, and Dudú lend themselves to distinction, *mutatis mutandis,* according to degree of bossiness, sensuality, and serene loveliness (see especially canto 6, sts. 40–54).

I would go so far as to suggest that the strategic placement of the female trios in *Don Juan* symbolizes the three modes of relationship that the protagonist may experience with women and through them with the world. Depending on the choice he makes, women (and his life) may become for him an experience of the graces, of the fates, or of the furies. In more abstract terms, Haidée-Aurora, suggesting the graces, would represent a timeless world formed of compassion, candor, and love; Julia-Fitz-Fulke, suggesting the fates, would represent a sensual world marked by brute repetition and monotony; and Gulbeyaz-Catherine-Lady Adeline, suggesting the furies, would represent an unfeeling but insatiable world characterized by exhausting duty and punishment. There is some indication that Juan feels he is put to choosing among the three women at Norman Abbey, and there is every indication that the narrator has a stake in the choice Juan makes; "I want a hero" is a tacit threat, though not a threat of force. Certainly the narrator chides Juan for finally choosing war over compassionate love, and slights him as the Empress Catherine's love-object, and confronts him with an explicit and unprecedented social-moral disapprobation after his sleeping in with the opportunistic Duchess.

This last episode generates a veritable hubbub of resonances. It not only shows Don Juan falling into the casual ways of the flesh, but shows this in the midst of one of his battles against superstition and terror (shades of the shipwreck episode). Where he should be wrestling with spirits, if not angels, he gets entangled in flesh. He is left unfit to meet the new day (Aurora) or even the ordinary world (A-munde-ville), having quite spent himself on the false spirit of darkness and concealed indulgence, and having left himself, as the poem observes with a telling Spenserian resonance, with "eyes that hardly brook'd / The light." The "air rebuk'd" in which the Duchess is seen also picks up the vocabulary of "virtue" and "vice" which Byron resorts to in this scene; its evaluative tone emerges markedly where Byron calls it an occasion for "Man to show his strength / Moral or physical." It is striking that where imagery of the Fall abounds in all previous love episodes, it is actually withheld and even opposed at this stage. For Byron carefully associates Aurora with a seraphic state and a possible recovery of Eden: "She look'd as if she sat at Eden's door. / And grieved for those who could return no more." It need not surprise us that she induces in Juan an unwonted "contemplation." She is, if Byron's pun may be spelled out, a cultivated Aurora who restores Haidée in a viable social mode, and not an idyllic, and perhaps idolatrous, isolation. She affords Juan the chance of a full new beginning, bringing to the poem "an ideal of womanhood attainable *within* society, though free from all its vices and illusions."

Two points may be brought into focus here. The first is what I would call the realistic humanism of this singular "non-epic" epic, which cannot consummate itself without a hero but whose hero, given opportunity and choice, seems to balk at a systematic heroism. Occasional heroism he is capable of, but he is betrayed into realism by his very capacity for heroism. To grapple with the Friar is to fall into the clutches of the Duchess of Fitz-Fulke. And we must observe that the narrator, though seeming to hope for more of his protagonist, knows human failing at first hand:

> If such doom [to be thought "Bores"] waits each intellectual Giant,
> We little people in our lesser way,
> In Life's small rubs should surely be more pliant,
> And so for one will I—as well I may—
> Would that I were less bilious—but, oh, fie on't!
> Just as I make my mind up every day
> To be a "totus, teres," Stoic, Sage,
> The wind shifts and I fly into a rage.
>
> (17.10)

Narrator and protagonist are not just separate figures in *Don Juan,* they are set at odds, one aspiring to stoicism and the other wavering between Aurora's purity ("beyond this world's perplexing waste") and the availability of her Frolic Grace, Fitz-Fulke. But both come together in being tripped out of the ideal. The "I want" which begins *Don Juan* and whose epic resonances may echo in the *cri de coeur* of Saul Bellow's Henderson, finally means both "I fail to discover, anywhere," and "I fail to become, anyhow" a hero. But it also means we are made to encounter, instead of the lyrical epic of Wordsworth's *The Prelude,* another innovation taking the form of an epical elegy tinged with a mythical or translunary vision. As Haidée and the Tartar Khan and even Aurora Raby show, we may not realistically expect a relation of more than nostalgia with that high world, of love and sacrifice and "a depth of feeling to embrace / Thoughts, boundless, deep, but silent too as Space." A shy leitmotif of elegy sets one of the amplitudes of *Don Juan.* The poem can make comedy of gothic terror, as in the Black Friar episode. But Byron is not kidding when he says that he laughed in order not to weep. The realistic humanism the poem displays is in this sense an achievement, not a dubious compromise. The poem constitutes the only place, between the procrustean magnitudes of traditional heroism and the procrustean diminishments of industrialism and imperialism, where mortal individualism has any play. "Between two worlds," Byron anticipates Arnold in saying

> life hovers like a star
> 'Twixt night and morn, upon the horizon's verge.
> How little do we know that which we are!
> How less what we may be! The eternal surge
> Of time and tide rolls on, and bears afar
> Our bubbles.
>
> (15.99)

To stay afloat is credit in itself, and in successive moments to defy the demon rum and deny a cannibalistic definition of human survival, and then to meet and mate Haidée constitute a life's achievement not to be sneered at. After this, of course, much is forgotten, even lost, and elegy supervenes on aspirations; but elegy, after all, is the tribute that mortality pays to the immortals of the erstwhile epic. And besides, it remains consolingly possible, with a sly shift of emphasis, "to laugh and make laugh."

The second point to focus on, in connection with the twofold pressure *Don Juan* exerts toward man's showing his strength, moral or physical, and his showing in the field of idealism and heroism, concerns less the tone of the poem than Byron's apparent freedom from formal or conventional constraints within it. I would like to suggest that every way he turns Byron manages to go in one direction. The way and the destination become, with each succeeding episode, increasingly difficult to sum up in a nutshell, but variations on the theme of physical and moral strength appear throughout. With this explicit theme, and with the narrator's infiltration into the poem's action, *Don Juan* becomes a generic hybrid of confession and satire, in epic guise. Confession and satire muffle each other, but both are based on a common preoccupation with the shortcomings of heroism. The play and the interplay of war and love, tyranny and individual fulfillment become the root concerns of the poem—its variety is tonal and modal, rather than substantial. Things and people do not stay long enough in the poem to change, it is true; instead they become one another, as war and love do in the person of the

Empress Catherine, as Spanish, Turkish, Russian, and English worlds become versions of one another, as love becomes the god of evil, as Donna Inez becomes Lambro becomes Gulbeyaz becomes Suwarrow becomes the Empress Catherine becomes Lady Adeline Amundeville, or as the Fall becomes a matter of Newtonian physics and humbler physiology and sexual rhythm (see canto 9, sts. 22, 45, 55), as well as wry allusion and social fortune and undifferentiated theology. And linking and imaging all this Don Juan becomes a part of all he sees and encounters.

In light of this mutual presence of classifiably separate things in each other, we may see a principle of association or ramification within the surface spontaneity and versatility of *Don Juan*. In fact we may argue a principle of unity based on obsession: Byron keeps coming back to one issue in various guises. The idea of obsession, startling though it may seem in relation to so sportively mannered a composition, does help to account for the reflexive repetitiousness of the poem, and may be necessary to account for any form of spontaneity, which after all expresses the unlabored capacity of a finite organism for response and action. One does most freely what one most fundamentally is bent to do. In literary terms we may see this also in Wordsworth's "spontaneous overflow of powerful feelings" that are carefully cultivated and also strongly, independently resurgent.

But the psychology of spontaneity and the quality of *Don Juan* require that more than this be said. The recurrence of obsession comes out here without its stagnancy and arrest. We can identify a pattern of enclosures in the poem and see that Don Juan falls deeper and deeper into prison or rather a realization of prison; his position changes though his situation remains roughly similar from his mother's house to Julia's tumbling bedroom to the ship *Trinidada* to Haidée's cave and Haidée's luxurious bedroom and the slave ship and the harem. Even this cursory catalogue makes it clear that Byron does more than repeat a certain setting and situation; he explores its forms and implications, and makes it into an instrument for apprehending and elucidating a human motif. In other words, as he goes back to it obsessively, he goes into it creatively; setting becomes an evolutionary symbol. Thus we can appreciate the irony of Juan's defying Gulbeyaz with his profession that love is for the free, and then literally fighting his way into the moral and physical subjection and exhaustion of the Empress Catherine's boudoir. The text moves from action to reflection to abstraction, though the protagonist may fail to keep pace.

In connection with this pattern of unfolding, enlarging, and altering identity in *Don Juan,* it should be of advantage to recall two cathedrals that figure prominently in the architectural symbolism of the romantic period: Wordsworth's "Gothic Cathedral" and Byron's "St. Peter's Basilica." The metaphor of Wordsworth's entire work as a Gothic cathedral conveys, beyond the immediate occasion of the preface to *The Excursion* (1814), his conception of all things as part of one; this is the conception that makes beginnings so difficult for Wordsworth ("Who knows the individual hour in which / His habits were first sown, even as a seed," when the mind, in "The words of Reason deeply weighed, / Hath no beginning"?).

It also makes ends chancy and imprecise for Wordsworth; the contribution any part makes to the whole stands beyond dispute, the vagueness or failure of every guide in *The Prelude* leaves every end in doubt and makes the poem nothing better than an exercise in frustrated teleology.

The metaphorization of St. Peter's in *Childe Harold,* canto 4 also serves to reveal, for the mind as well as for poetry, a process of indefinite epistemological development; like Zeno's traveler, one gets closer to a total comprehension of things met piecemeal, without ever quite getting there. "Thou movest," Byron writes of the reverent visitor whose mind "Has grown colossal":

>   —but increasing with the advance,
> Like climbing some great Alp, which still doth rise,
> Deceived by its gigantic elegance;
> Vastness which grows, but grows to harmonise—
> All musical in its immensities;
> Rich marbles, richer painting, shrines where flame
> The lamps of gold, and haughty dome which vies
> In air with Earth's chief structures, though their frame
> Sits on the firm-set ground—and this the clouds must claim.
>
> Thou seest not all; but piecemeal thou must break
> To separate contemplation the great whole;
> And as the ocean many bays will make,
> That ask the eye—so here condense thy soul
> To more immediate objects, and control
> Thy thoughts until thy mind hath got by heart
> Its eloquent proportions, and unroll
> In mighty graduations, part by part,
> The glory which at once upon thee did not dart,

> Not by its fault—but thine. Our outward sense
> Is but of gradual grasp: and as it is
> That what we have of feeling most intense
> Outstrips our faint expression; even so this
> Outshining and o'erwhelming edifice
> Fools our fond gaze, and greatest of the great
> Defies at first our Nature's littleness,
> Till, growing with its growth, we thus dilate
> Our spirits to the size of that they contemplate
> (4.156–58)

It would seem fair to infer, on the strength of these two cathedral metaphors, that the character of infinity does not belong to the poem as physical object, but rather to the pursuit of the object—the world and our experience of it—which the poem embodies. And it is important to acknowledge the obverse of the ever-expanding circuit of Byron's interest, namely, his own awareness of the tremendous intricacy of what seems small. Such intricacy results in a kind of expansion inward; as Byron writes in "The Dream," "in itself a thought, / A slumbering thought is capable of years, / And curdles a long life into one hour." This principle of immense miniaturization is illustrated in *Don Juan*, canto 8, stanzas 56–59, where Lascy and Juan reenact the Tower of Babel; Byron summarizes as follows:

> And therefore all we have related in
> Two long octaves, pass'd in a little minute;
> But in the same small minute, every sin
> Contrived to get itself comprised within it.
> The very cannon, deafen'd by the din,
> Grew dumb, for you might almost hear a linnet,
> As soon as thunder, 'midst the general noise
> Of Human Nature's agonizing voice!

The passage has a severely cryptic quality and is full of images yearning to be heard, like Juan or a linnet; but we may note that a cannon and an agonizing voice, though these are at top decibel, also fail to be heard, indicating a moral rather than an acoustical problem. The little minute contains more than every sin; it contains everything by implication, and it would seem that the poem gets larger, as by authorial commentary, not only to encompass a polyglot universe in a single aesthetic space, but also to enunciate the wealth of implication in that universe's single objects. The use of allusion, so prevalent in the poem, thus deserves special notice as a form of bringing various worlds, of time and thought and value, into concert around a given, ostensibly isolated moment.

The mode of development of *Don Juan*—"now and then narrating, / Now pondering"—clearly reinforces the techniques of turning obsession into a disciplined instrument of creative insight. The action themes of war and love consort with the contemplative motifs of skepticism and humanism. In short, the poem is thinking its action, through itself, fusing obsession and philosophy, incident and teleology. We should note that, after the adventitiousness of the shipwreck and arrival on Haidée's island, the sequence of incidents right up to the landing in England is very closely linked together, almost becoming a causal chain in the teeth of the casual emergency system that seems to prevail.

It is necessary to go beyond the patterning of moments and characters if we are to realize the full aesthetic discipline and shapeliness underlying the free play of *Don Juan*. There operates in the poem in idiocratic (or self-determining) action and rhythm, whereby it becomes remarkably consistent and lucid and weighty and significant in form. This action and rhythm may well derive from Byron's life, and to that extent may resemble a helpless or mechanically obsessive occurrence, but it is generalized and abstracted to meet extra-biographical, catholic needs, and so must be taken as a matter of artistic choice and deployment.

This is, of course, the action and rhythm that we recognize in all the major episodes of *Don Juan*; it first appears in the Juan-Julia episode, which I have accordingly signalized as prototypal, and it comprises five main elements:

1. an authority figure (Donna Inez, Lambro, Gulbeyaz, the Empress Catherine, Lady Adeline Amundeville) who more or less directly contributes to the development of a profane or wrong action;

2. initial passivity or dependency on the protagonist's part, though he exerts a powerful attraction and possesses great potential energy;

3. a clandestine affair of love softly, almost inadvertently, begun, and with strong hints of exaltation;

4. a realistic redefinition of that love, with a burst of violence and a threat to the protagonist's life;

5. the protagonist's renewed subjugation, to force rather than to authority, and his ensuing exile, a period of reflection and evaluation.

The elaboration of this idiocratic structure in *Don Juan* affords a sense of stability in the poem, but would be harmful if it implied any sort of stagnation. Rather the dynamism of the poem is invested in this

structure, which grows increasingly subtle and reverberative and reve-
latory of the poem's values. Thus, for example, the exile from Haidée's
island constitutes more of a spiritual loss than the initial exile from Spain,
though Spain is technically home (the homelessness and nostalgia running
through the poem are not geographical but spiritual); the superior value
of Haidée's world to Julia's is manifest in Juan's naturally and nobly
remembering Haidée's, as opposed to the fate of the missive with which
Julia pursues him.

In short the contours, the textures, the values of the elements in the
idiocratic structure of *Don Juan* significantly alter as we proceed. Perhaps
the most elusive and most complicated instance occurs at the Russian
court, which will repay a closer scrutiny. There is some justice in beginning at the end of canto 8, where Juan makes a vow "which," Byron
emphasizes, "he kept," to shield the Moslem orphan, Leila. She, like
Aurora to come, is one of the homeless in the text, but we may see more
significance in the ways she calls Haidée back to mind; for, like Haidée's,
Leila's entire world, her family and her very place of birth, have "per-
ished." But she survives, and Juan, albeit purblindly, may be regarded
here as preserving something which the poem at any rate associates with
Haidée. It is an authentic act, but it continues to exist in the framework
of Byron's earlier question: "What's this in one annihilated city?" The
dominant energy resides with war, not compassion, and Juan approaches
the Empress Catherine's court as a man capable of occasional good but,
as Virgil says of warriors, intoxicated with blood.

It is ominous that Donna Inez reenters the poem here for the first
and only time, to give her maternal sanction to the "maternal affection"
the Empress Catherine bears Don Juan, just as she had earlier fostered
Donna Julia's "platonic" affection for him. In fact the confusion of love
and bad poetry and humor and war that exists in Catherine's soul (and
which stands embodied in Juan artificially accoutred as "Love turned a
Lieutenant of Artillery") is compounded by the identification of the do-
mestic and political power and by the disguise of raw imperious lust in
the cloak of benevolence. A kind of metaphysical chaos is dissimulated
by the splendor of the court and the recent victory, but its perversity
finally appears in the very form of its disguise—if the Empress Catherine
is maternal, she is the mother who consumes her own children, and
consumes them incestuously. This, of course, focuses her in opposition
to Haidée, the "mother" who saves Juan and whose dreams, however
harrowing to herself, imply an infinite capacity for saving, if not giving,

life. A further sign of chaos resides in the fact that when all is said and done, the Empress Catherine functions at once as Donna Inez, as Donna Julia, and as Don Alfonso—as instigator, paramour, and punisher in this escapade. The height of Juan's reputation becomes the height of confusion and, indeed, of degradation. It is not surprising that "he grew sick," in body and spirit. Catherine of course tries to save him, and we have the final irony and confusion of the entire episode, namely, that the purported cure is designed to prolong the disease and may endanger his life. A gracious but effectual exile ensues.

Juan here reaches the nadir of his career. But there are good, or at least hopeful, signs. Leila, with all the benevolence that she attracts, firmly frames the episode at the Russian court, and as she heads for England over land and sea with Juan a significant positive temper springs up in him. I have suggested above that the exile scenes serve as intervals of reflection and evaluation. In each Juan has one main companion: Pedrillo, the tutor manqué; Johnson, the worldly-wise man whose wisdom is not à propos and whose skin is really saved by Juan; and now Leila. With Leila there is no uncertainty as to who is protecting whom. Juan, coming off his worst subjugation and most essential defeat in the poem, begins to recover himself as a magnanimous man. Clear and viable relationships begin to crystallize again, and even as the English scene looms ahead, wheeling like swords about his so-called virgin-face, it seems that in Aurora Raby he can find the three crucial relationships Comte says man bears to woman: that of veneration, as for a mother; of attachment, as for a wife; of benevolence, as for a child. Here is the relationship of wholeness that opposes the relationship of chaos we have seen in the case of the Empress Catherine. These relationships have partially existed, or perversely appeared, before. Now, having gone through them, however imperfectly, and having reflected on them, however incidentally, he is in a position to commit himself and satisfy the soul of the man who cannot but "want a hero."

It is only by the structure of the poem, with its discovery of the critical value of obsession and of self-discipline in an unconventional spontaneity, that such a position has been reached. And it is in turn what I have called the realistic humanism of the poem—a compound of plangent skepticism and sardonic merriment and undying dreams of human magnificence—that makes this position so hard to resolve. The poem falls somewhere between the picaresque and the bildungsroman, and so, perhaps, Don Juan becomes, more even than Wordsworth, the romantic hero of everyday, whose occasions and whose aspirations lead him to a transcendental Haidée and Aurora, while yet his occasions and his impulses involve him with hoary Empresses who stand for old Glory and indiscriminate primitive modes of love.

Byron's *Don Juan:*
Myth as Psychodrama

Candace Tate

In his "uncommon want" of a hero, Byron deliberately chose Don Juan as one whose myth satisfied his own needs both as poet and as private man. Examining Byron's poetic reworking of the Don Juan myth in relation to his own psychology yields a reading that lends continuity to a poem still being termed a "hold-all." The myth is descended from Tirso de Molina's *El burlador de Sevilla y convidado de piedra* (ca. 1616), which combines an account of the amorous adventures of a fictive character whom Tirso named Don Juan, with the Spanish folktale of a stone statue that comes to life and delivers the village rogue to hell. Both the amorous adventures of the Don and the avenging stone statue are central to Byron's presentation of the myth.

The classical, or pre-romantic, Don Juan is renowned more for his ceaseless efforts than for his actual triumphs. He resorts to all sorts of chicanery: even his successes tend to be comically colored by the over-intensity of his assaults. The Byronic Don Juan, on the other hand, is *l'homme fatal,* universally irresistible. The humor in Byron's *Don Juan* is provided only by the narrative voice. The narrator's skillful, satiric assaults upon humanity's sacrosanct foibles are counterpoised against the inadvertent quality of Juan's successes. The narrator jokes about Juan's innocence, but his tone remains light and playful when he speaks of him. The egoistic exuberance of the young Don's adventures contrasts with the diabolical character of the traditional Don, whose famed selfish, blus-

From *Keats-Shelley Journal* 29 (1980). © 1980 by Keats-Shelley Association of America, Inc.

tering cynicism Byron makes an attribute of the knowing narrator, rather
than of his naive hero. In a sense, the cynical wisdom of the narrator is
what the naive Juan is evolving toward throughout the poem. In fact,
Byron seems to have created an entirely new version of the myth: he has
given Juan the characteristic erotic prowess, but he leaves him unchar-
acteristically vulnerable to women. Juan's virility is not only subject to
the taming influence of love, it is also coveted, manipulated, and subjugated by every female he encounters.

Similarly, in the traditional versions of the legend, Don Juan's insult
to the spirit of the dead *commandante* animates the stone statue, and his
defiance becomes the final offense for which all his lechery is punished;
the last scene of fiery annihilation is appropriately heroic. Yet, the personality of Byron's Don Juan, by contrast, seems to fade, and the narrator
becomes dominant just as the poem comes to a fragmented conclusion.

Juan's encounter with the lady ghost, and the disastrous effects of
their night together—their mutual fatigue, the implications that sex as
the ultimate sensation leaves Juan depleted and dissatisfied—completes
Byron's irascible interpretation of the myth: the libertine who holds out
his hand to specters or avenging spirits is inviting consummation, especially if his bedchamber is on hallowed ground. While the traditional
Don Juan is visited by a stone statue from a monastery, and is consumed
by flames, Byron's Don Juan is visited by a live woman simply disguised
as the ghost of a friar and is annihilated by sexual consummation. Com-
bining the memories of his own childhood terror of Newstead Abbey
with the pattern of the original myth, Byron thus makes Juan the unfortunate prey of the restless ghost who haunts Norman Abbey in retribution of offenses the Amundevilles are still committing against the
"glorious remnant of the Gothic pile," and the statues of the "Twelve
saints [which] had once stood sanctified in stone." The offense against
the statues is integral to the animation of the Byronic specter, and, in
conformity to the traditional version of the myth, it is the crime for which
the Don receives his ultimate punishment. His sexual energy is totally
enveloped by female aggression. The legend of the Black Friar of Norman
Abbey is a hoax, but so, in Byron's poem, is the myth of Don Juan's
inexhaustible, indomitable sexuality. In fact, in Byron's version of the
legend women are fatal to Juan; sex is anathema, and he is too enchanted
with his own image to see the joke.

The neat reversals of the traditional elements of the legend indicate
that Byron's poem does more than recast the *burlador* as romantic hero.
The narrator of the poem is ostensibly concerned with judging society

in terms of romantic idealism, but the poet is ultimately concerned with the etiology and evolution of Juan's delusions. The poem scrutinizes the pathology of being human. Everyone, including Juan, capitalizes on his charismatic sexuality. Juan is the key to the poem, yet he is only significant in relation to the other characters. The pattern of his relationships with other characters is essentially one of relationships with women and their men, established in canto 1 and repeated throughout the poem. While traditional criticism says Byron makes small use of the Don Juan myth, the pattern of Don Juan's relationship with women and their men does, in fact, conform throughout the poem to the patterns of the original myth, but turned about for purposes that a psychoanalytic examination of the poem will clarify. The hero seems deliberately depicted as the personification of the Don Juan complex, as described by Otto Fenichel more than a century later:

> Don Juan's behavior is no doubt due to his Oedipus complex. He seeks his mother in all women and cannot find her. But the analysis of Don Juan types shows that their Oedipus complex is of a particular kind. It is dominated by the pregenital aim of incorporation, pervaded by narcissistic needs and tinged with sadistic impulses. . . . The striving for sexual satisfaction is still condensed with the striving for getting narcissistic supplies in order to maintain self-esteem. . . . His narcissistic need requires proof of his ability to excite women; after he knows that he is able to excite a specific woman, his doubts arise concerning other women whom he has not yet tried.
>
> [*The Psychoanalytic Theory of Neuroses*]

Incorporation, or the infantile desire to engulf external objects, is the Don Juan personality's habitual response toward women: he sees sexual conquest as a means of reunion with the omnipotent external force that mother represents; yet, he also fears this reunion because of a concomitant fantasy of being engulfed by it—hence the oedipal relationship carries "a frequent and intense unconscious connection between the ideas of sexuality and death," between sexuality and an anticipation of retribution. As a result of his conformity to the Don Juan complex, Juan emerges as the least mobile character in the drama. Byron employs him in a particular role, with a severely limited repertoire of responses.

Given that Byron invented neither the Don Juan myth, nor the Don Juan complex, he does devote considerable effort to dramatizing the phenomenon. Byron himself was a man with a compulsion for self-dramatization, and the term "psychodrama," the reenactment of problematic past experiences, real or imagined, in an effort to resolve them, may well express what the poem was for Byron. By concentrating on Juan and the ladies, we can see how the poem served the poet as a kind of therapeutic theater in which he could reenact certain of his own problematic amorous adventures—such as incest both real and fancied—in an attempt to achieve relief from the anxiety that memory must perpetuate. The creation of *Don Juan* was Byron's attempt to fuse conflicting elements of his own personality, as well as those of the myth he had become:

> They made me, without my search, a species of popular Idol; they, without reason or judgement, beyond the caprice of their good pleasure, threw down the Image from its pedestal; it was not broken with the fall, and they would, it seems, again replace it—but they shall not.

He wrote this letter, as he wrote *Don Juan,* in exile, and both are public statements of hubris that refute the powers of social retribution. Byron was concerned with the reader's reaction to *Don Juan* only insofar as it related to his own need to be accepted as a Don Juan: Byron reserves judgment for himself, and the poem as psychodrama will reveal that his Nemesis, like Juan's, is a form of degraded eroticism which he may describe or reenact, but which he will not, cannot deny.

Freud's statement about the poet's relation to his work is fundamental to our understanding of Byron's undertaking:

> Some actual experience which made a strong impression on the writer had stirred up a memory of an earlier experience, generally belonging to childhood, which then arouses a wish that finds a fulfillment in the work in question, and in which elements of the recent event and the old memory should be discernible. [*On Creativity and The Unconscious: Papers on the Psychology of Art, Literature, Love, and Religion*]

Throughout the poem, we can see elements of Byron's childhood, his marriage and divorce, and the trauma of his relationship with Augusta Leigh interwoven into Juan's adventures. If we expand upon Freud, using Moreno's principles of psychodrama, however, according to which the actor (who is also the author) in this genre is the protagonist, and all the other characters in the poem represent "auxiliary egos," actors who "play the roles of absent people involved in his problems or fears" [Ira A. Greenberg, *Psychodrama and Audience Attitude Change*], canto 1, as a deliberate innovation to the traditional Don Juan myth, is doubly significant then: we can see the poet's overt attempt to create a plausible source of Juan's eventual disorder, and Byron's own oedipal problems emerge as the ultimate conflict in his psychodrama, with Juan as the protagonist of myth and psychodrama both.

The evolution of Juan as a character spans the wealth of the poem, linking Byron's playful treatment of the sensuous innocent to his portrait of the weary *cavalier servente* of English drawing-room society. Byron devotes most attention to Juan's psychological development in canto 1, through the detailed description of Juan's childhood behavior and adolescent sensibility. While the Russian cantos make some reference to Juan's dissipation and a mysterious illness, it is only within the confines of Norman Abbey (cantos 12–17) that Byron returns to an in-depth scrutiny of the hero and once again explores the psychology of his malaise. Though the entire poem, particularly such episodes as those of Haidée, Juan, and Lambro, bears examination in terms of Byron's psychodrama, these cantos will serve to illustrate the ways in which Byron's own psychology informs his reinterpretation of the myth.

The poet points out that the seeds of Juan's discontent were started in Seville. His mother, like Byron's, is repression personified: "Some women use their tongues—she *looked* a lecture" (1.15.1). His father is a henpecked cavalier, "a mortal of the careless kind" (1.19.1), whose indiscreet love affairs prove his undoing. According to the narrator, Donna Inez becomes incensed by the gossip and begins to torment her husband:

> But then she had a devil of a spirit
> And sometimes mixed up fancies with realities,
> And let few opportunities escape
> Of getting her liege lord into a scrape.
>
> (1.20.5–8)

Juan is doted upon, yet undisciplined, because his parents are distracted by maintaining conduct that is "exceedingly well-bred," while "Wishing each other, not divorced, but dead" (1.26.3). Inez attempts to dispose of José by proving him insane, but, lacking enough evidence, she settles for divorce, gathering the forces of public opinion to do battle against her husband:

> The hearers of her case became repeaters,
> Then advocates, inquisitors, and judges,
> Some for amusement, others for old grudges.
>
> (1.28.6–8)

With the added enforcement of social institutions, Inez's actual wish is
fulfilled:

> The lawyers did their utmost for divorce,
> But scarce a fee was paid on either side
> Before, unluckily, Don José died.
>
> (1.32.6–8)

Don José, like Byron, is doomed because his own "malus animus"
prevents him from understanding his wife's pernicious hypocrisy; José is
too busy pursuing his pleasures to realize that under her cultivated air of
stoic magnanimity, she has never ceased plotting revenge. In the contest
of wills, Donna Inez's triumphs; José's physical and spiritual strength are
destroyed:

> Standing alone beside his desolate hearth,
> Where all his household gods lay shivered round him.
> No choice was left his feeling or his pride,
> Save death or Doctors' Commons—so he died.
>
> (1.36.5–8)

His power, his life force as symbolized by the household gods, is broken.
The shattered gods, the desolate hearth, are touching images of depleted
forms that once held life but now are cold, empty, and powerless. His
death wish toward Inez, his magic, was no match for hers.

The chronicle of Don José and Donna Inez's divorce parallels Byron's
own, but the actual death of José relates to the death of Byron's father,
Captain John Byron:

> George was three and one-half years old when his father died,
> and less than three when he saw him for the last time, but he
> later told Thomas Medwin: "I was not so young when my
> father died, but that I perfectly remember him; and had very
> early a horror of matrimony, from the sight of domestic broils.
> . . . He seemed born for his own ruin, and that of the other
> sex."
>
> [*Byron: A Biography*, Leslie A. Marchand]

Mrs. Byron "assuaged her passionate grief by a mingled hatred and love
of the son who reminded her of . . . [her husband]" [Marchand]. Un-
fortunately for Byron, he was too early the man of the house, like Juan
"An only son left with an only mother" (1.37.7).

Juan is left to Inez's care. She proceeds to discipline and shape his education, "Resolved that Juan should be quite a paragon, / And worthy of the noblest pedigree" (1.38.2–3). The futility of her excessive effort is intimated even in this early description of Juan's education: Juan's pedigree naturally includes José's legacy, what Inez's lawyers call a propensity for evil, and "paragon" implies excellence, but it is morally vague. Because of these earliest accounts of Juan's curriculum, his virtue is made something to joke about; one realizes from the narrator's sly remarks that Donna Inez cannot quite maintain control, and tension builds as Juan matures.

Byron shows Juan approaching manhood, amid the screaming protests of Donna Inez, and the docile machinations of Donna Julia. The "almost man" is thrilled and confused with Donna Julia, ignorant of the cause of these new feelings. The narrator vacillates between hinting that something "From sire to son to augur good or ill" is a scandalous possibility, and claiming that Juan is aware of something, but cannot imagine that it could be a "Thing quite in course, and not at all alarming, / Which with a little patience might grow charming" (1.86.7–8). Juan as "Poor little fellow!" is incredibly dumb. He wanders, "silent and pensive," through the woods—in fact, he wanders through the entire canto without ever uttering a word. He is purportedly only aware of Julia's eyes, and even this conscious longing occurs in the midst of metaphysical ponderings. He is lost for hours to his scrutiny of leaves and flowers, hearing "a voice in all the winds," filled with imaginings of wood nymphs and "how the goddesses came down to men." These gentle, pensive imaginings of Juan's are sublimated erotic longings. The imagery couches his sexuality in such a manner as to make it palatable to the reader. By thus engaging the reader's approval of Juan's budding sexual appetite, Byron appears to be reshaping the symbol of Don Juan as the comically overassertive lecher, to that of a wandering innocent whose passion is linked to wood nymphs and goddesses. Juan's somnambulant sexuality is given a preternatural quality, which is essentially the characteristic that explains his appeal for women throughout the poem.

In contrast to Juan's passionate ignorance, Julia's knowing attempts at self-control appear contrived and ludicrous:

> Yet Julia's very coldness still was kind,
> And tremulously gentle her small hand
> Withdrew itself from his, but left behind.
> (1.71.1–3)

> She vow'd she never would see Juan more
> And next day paid a visit to his mother.
> (1.76.1–2)

She has prayed to the Virgin Mary as "the best judge of a lady's case," but, when she misses seeing Juan, the Virgin is "no further prayed." Her turmoil is declared in terms of a Christian's inner struggle, that of the virtuous wife tempted by the devil "so very sly," amidst "love divine," angels, and "reveries celestial." Her serenity, however, has a certain concupiscent smugness to it: deciding that her honor is "a rock or a mole," she dispenses "with any kind of troublesome control." She envisions a plan that makes provision for her husband's death, while it ingeniously allows her to begin immediate instruction of Juan in "the rudiments of love."

Julia's fantasy about Alfonso's death exactly resembles Inez's death wish toward José:

> And if in the meantime her husband died,
> But heaven forbid that such a thought should cross
> Her brain, though in a dream, and then she sighed.
> (1.84.1–3)

As Inez's social and psychological peer, Julia becomes a parental substitute for Juan; as another character in Byron's psychodrama, she embodies again his own mother's violent hatred toward her husband and the emotional excesses that her stern Presbyterian principles neither disciplined, nor relieved, but as with Julia, and Inez, hatred is nicely submerged beneath a veneer of respectability, and the hated husband is replaced by the more easily dominated son.

Byron has been pointing at similarities between Inez and Julia since he first introduced Julia into Inez's domain. The narrator imputes scandal to be the basis of their friendship. If "Inez had, ere Don Alfonso's marriage, / Forgot with him her very prudent carriage" (1.66.7–8), and in "still keeping up the old connexion . . . / She took his lady also in affection" (1.67.1,3), then Julia's fifty-year-old husband, as Inez's lover, doubles as a father figure to both Julia and Juan, and the implication is, of course, that the young pair could be sister and brother. Alfonso's relationship with Inez and the chance of his being Juan's actual father, or at least old enough to substitute as the father symbol in the exclusive "only mother," "only son" affiliation, sets up an oedipal configuration between these three characters, which is further complicated by the possibility that Julia is "sister-mother" to Juan. When she is depicted as the young wife of a "jealous lord," innocently caressing Juan, this passes as a kind of youthful familiarity. The psychic consanguinity becomes more complex, however, as she assumes the role of older woman, guiding him into a forbidden affair: then, her role as knowing voluptuary and Juan's as the sexually precocious child set the stage for the inevitable confrontation between father-Alfonso and Juan.

Whereas in his own childhood Byron never actually confronted his father, he would have shared his mother's guilt, that is, he would have been aware that his exclusive attachment to her psychologically demanded his complicity in the death wish she expressed toward his father. His relationship with Augusta Leigh was similar to Juan's relationship with Julia and Inez: the sister displaces the mother in an incestuous relationship that could be actualized, and the guilt and anxiety that his father's death had left with him would be resolved by the punishment the incest would inevitably incur.

The confrontation scene is the only aspect of Juan's and Julia's affair that Byron concerns himself with. After so long and carefully preparing the seduction, he devotes only a few lines to their enjoyment; the conflict and upheaval are far more dramatically significant. Their passion is mentioned only briefly, amid the comings and goings of the chagrined Alfonso, and with the maid standing around to chastise their foolishness. The lovers together are never allowed to achieve the grandeur with which they are comically endowed as individual characters. Juan is still the *enfant terrible,* the naughty man-child, while Julia has developed into a fabliau harpy, the nasty mother-figure capable of holding her own in their struggle with the cuckolded Alfonso. The incestuous implications of stanzas 9 through 117 are no longer strained and snide. The maid, Antonia, gives an indirect praise of Juan that makes the contrast between Julia, the knowing dowager, and Juan, the precocious child, humorous:

> "Had it but been for a stout cavalier
> Of twenty-five or thirty (Come, make haste)
> But for a child, what piece of work is here!
> I really, madam, wonder at your taste."
>
> (1.172.1–4)

"Stout" has some nice phallic qualities, and the phrase "piece of work" quite explains Julia's "taste." Compared to poor old Alfonso, whose "sword had dropp'd ere he could draw it," and who comes off the impotent buffoon of the scene, Juan is the virile figure who is all the less culpable because he cannot quite pull off the escapade. All he inflicts on Alfonso is a bloody nose, as he runs off naked into the night. Whatever damage Juan has done to Alfonso's sexual nose is innocuous, and the potentially dangerous scene is farcically resolved. For Byron, canto 1 allows him to recreate through fantasy, and memory, the bizarre relationships with his own overprotective mother, and wife, and to joke about his own oedipal, or sister-mother, relationship with Augusta Leigh. His treatment of these ladies within the context of the poem is also integral to the turnabout he makes upon the traditional Don Juan myth: the Don cannot alter his fate: it is conceived and delivered by women.

Byron's method of handling Julia's sexuality merits some further explication, because it prefigures his pattern of developing females as paradoxically predictable and mysterious. While Julia's soft sighs are actually expressions of a powerful erotic appetite, Byron's laughing exaggeration of her feigned restraint, in terms of the Christian metaphor, makes her seem only silly. Yet, as the source of Juan's sexual initiation and the cause of his exile, her sexuality becomes threatening. She claims little of the reader's sympathy; stanzas of her farewell letter to Juan are touching, but the sentiment is immediately undercut by the narrator's description of the care with which the adieu is prepared—even her sorrow seems contrived; her tragedy is mere melodrama. Julia is important as Juan's first lover because she embodies all the puzzling aspects with which Byron endows women throughout Juan's adventures:

> Oh thou *teterrima causa* of all *belli*—
> Thou gate of life and death—thou nondescript!
> Whence is our exit and our entrance. Well I
> May pause in pondering how all souls are dipt
> In thy perennial fountain. How man fell, I
> Know not, since knowledge saw her branches stript
> Of her first fruit; but how he falls and rises
> Since, thou hast settled beyond all surmises.
>
> (9.55.1–8)

> Some call thee "the worst cause of war," but I
> Maintain thou art the best, for after all
> From thee we come, to thee we go.
>
> (9.56.1–3)

Because they are a mystery, all women represent an external threat to Juan's sexuality, and Byron needs Juan to enact an escape from their motherly manipulations. Juan's role as the "innocent" in canto 1 differentiates him from the traditional Don Juan character: he is the conquered, not the conqueror, and the parallel between the two heroes' adventures does not clearly emerge until the English cantos. Here, Byron fulfills the prophecy that he is writing about the same hero of the pantomimes, plays, and operas. The English episodes illustrate that Byron has kept the legend of Don Juan and the stone guest within his overall poetic design. With "new mythological machinery, / And very handsome supernatural scenery" (1.201.7–8) he will manage "in canto twelfth . . . to show / The very place where wicked people go" (1.207.7–8).

The Don Juan of the English episodes impresses us with the dispassionate savoir-faire he has learned in Russia. In contrast to the fabulous description within which Byron couched Juan's adolescent fantasies in canto 1, with its apotheosis of Juan's innocent eroticism, the itinerary of Juan's advance into the aristocratic circles of London appears merely matter-of-fact. He is the "young diplomatic sinner" who has come to England to regain his health after the dissipation that he was enjoying in Russia mysteriously made him sick. The narrator suggests the cause was "the Empress's *maternal* [my italics] love" (10.32.8), because even as Juan did "his duty, / In royalty's vast arms he sighed for beauty" (10.37.7–8). Like the youth of canto 1, Juan barely escapes the dowager's engulfing embrace, but in the Russian canto Byron seems to be suggesting that Juan is becoming somewhat of a predator himself, because the "imperious passion," which Juan dedicates to Catherine in canto 9, is the "self-love" that makes Juan believe himself "as good as any" (9.68.8).

We see him approaching the throne with a predetermined intent to serve the queen in a particular fashion. Like Byron, Juan has become a *cavalier servente*; these cantos were written while the poet was "settled into regular *serventismo*" to Teresa Guiccioli, and Byron's own ambivalence about his servitude is reflected in his delineation of Juan's Russian post:

> What were the actual and official duties
> Of the strange thing some women set a value on,
> Which hovers oft about some married beauties,
> Called *cavalier servente*—a Pygmalion
> Whose statues warm
>
> . . . .
> Beneath his art.
>
> (9.51.2–7)

Whatever his official duties were in Russia, this equation of women to statues who animate under his art has foreboding implications, both in relation to Juan's oedipal relationship to Catherine, and as a *figura* of the stone statue that comes to life and punishes Don Juan's lechery in the traditional myth: we would expect Byron to demand punishment from an aroused female statue, because of his own oedipal problems, and Juan's strange malady in Russia is yet another way in which the poet expresses his neurosis.

Since Byron's own displaced oedipal problem, his relationship with Augusta Leigh, is integral to his memories of England, by calling England hell in his version of the legend, and by demonstrating the omnivorous immorality of the aristocracy, the government, and the business magnates, he is attempting to invalidate the social condemnation that had forced his exile. Byron's idea of "the place where wicked people go," hell as expressed in canto 12, is simultaneously different from and identical to the traditional Don Juan's destination. In a letter to Murray, written after the completion of canto 5, he claims that he has "not quite fixed whether to make . . . Juan end in Hell, or in an unhappy marriage, not knowing which would be the severest." His next remark about the tradition seems good evidence that he is still keeping the traditional legend well in mind: "The Spanish tradition says Hell: but it is probably only an Allegory of the other state." Hence, Juan's "last elopement with the devil" should conform to Byron's conscious interpretation of the traditional legend, as well as being part of the poet's psychodrama and reflective of his unconscious interpolations of the elements of the myth: the word "elopement" in connection with the "devil" points again toward Byron's connection of punishment with the wife-mother figure. Marriage is inherently bound to his transgression of the incest taboo. For the traditional libertine, marriage is an "Allegory" of hell because it represents external restrictions upon his own desire to engulf the objective world. The traditional Don is the aggressor; in London, Byron's Juan is still the obliging son-lover, whose hell is a continuum of falls, with sister-mother.

The epic similes of canto 10 prepare the reader for a more spectacular hell than Juan encounters in canto 12, yet the true map of Juan's descent does underlie Byron's description of his first view of London:

> The sun went down, the smoke rose up, as from
> A half-unquenched volcano, o'er a space

> Which well beseemed the "devil's drawing room,"
> As some have qualified that wondrous place.
>
> (10.81.14)

Byron's metaphor of London refers to "the popular tradition that craters of volcanoes lead directly to the pit of hell, hence to the devil's drawing-room" (W. W. Pratt, Notes to the Penguin edition, 1973). The "pit of hell" in canto 12 is London, and the "Smithfield Show" a flesh market where all the members of drawing-room society survey each other in an endless parade of possible marriage bargains. Juan enters London, the "devil's drawing-room," with little hesitation; he hovers "undecided / Amongst the paths of being 'taken in,'" pausing only long enough to be received into the "best" society. Whereas the belching infernos of canto 11 and the repeated references within that canto to London as "damned" would seem to be setting the scene for our hero to enter a fiery hell—to meet death in submission or defiance, according to the heroic *burlador* tradition—perdition becomes only a metaphor of the change in Juan's psychology. In canto 12, hell is an experience that polishes the skills he had begun to acquire in Russia, and Juan's resemblance to the traditional libertine becomes apparent: he has learned to see women as objects whom he may desire and engulf. He learns to maneuver within the social market-place, only hesitating "at *first* because he did not think the women pretty." Like a mercantile Narcissus, he sees his own worth as a reflection of others' desires, and he proceeds to shop for a lady worthy of his charms. In canto 12, our hero has wandered into an existential hell, where reality is the bartering experience endlessly perpetuated, and universally perpetrated. The narrator lambasts society; Byron refuses to differentiate between Juan and mankind. While the narrator delivers scathing descriptions of genial hypocrisy, Byron shows Juan indulging in the same peccadilloes. Juan is doomed to the ordinary, and in London he seems shallow and insignificant without his mythical trappings.

At the close of canto 12, Juan has been left "exposed to temptation," but then Byron has done this to him so often that one does not take the narrator seriously when he insists on repeating it. The reader can see that Juan has developed a social cunning that makes the most of any occasion, and the defenseless man-child of the first canto has developed at last into the libertine after whom he is named: he no longer stands "in the predicament / Of a mere novice." His experience, his past servitude, seems to have equipped him to handle even "The loveliest oligarchs of our gynocracy." For Byron, the "English setting makes the last cantos, stanza for stanza, more personal than the preceding ten" [Truman Guy Steffan, *The Making of a Masterpiece: Byron's Don Juan,* vol. 1 of *Byron's* Don Juan: *A Variorum Edition*], and he uses Juan to reenact the dynamics of his own social triumphs in England. The atmosphere is melancholic, however, and Juan seems to have settled into a "dreary void," an abyss of the "polished, smooth, and cold." The women are lewdly voracious, "marble," and "ice," another collection of cool statues, with an assortment of cuckolded husbands.

The Don Juan of the last English cantos is only a bored aristocrat whose sense of malaise seems part of the social disease he contracted in canto 12. He is a sophisticated strategist, managing to keep one step ahead of Adeline and her matriarchal machinations. In fact, up until canto 16, it appears that Byron is going to ignore the traditional confrontation between Don Juan and the devil that he promised the reader in canto 1. Juan's offenses hardly seem to merit an avenging specter. Instead, Byron has shown that the betrayals are done by the women upon their husbands, and any shame they incur, they bear as emblems of the pleasure they knew with Juan. They never curse Juan or call upon their husbands or heaven to avenge their honor—the image of the ladies' being usually too busy plotting revenge upon their husbands is one of Byron's favorite and most autobiographical motifs. Byron's *cavalier servente* does receive a few curses from the husbands, or even from a father or two, but since immorality is ubiquitous in his version of the libertine's life and loves, their curses are a comic bluster, part of the overall social satire. Juan lacks the braggadocio that would force the comparison between his own fame as it is discussed in England and the renowned lechery of the legendary Don. The ordinary quality of Juan's dissipation and his sharing this doom daily with his peers leave the reader unprepared for any hell but a continuation of the ennui that has plagued our hero for six cantos.

Thus, when Byron creates a ghost at Norman Abbey, and refers to the curse of the Amundevilles, the family's offense to the stone statues, there would appear to be no connection to Juan or the ghost who leads Don Juan to hell in the stone guest legend. Juan's anxieties appear to be focused on Aurora's "self-possession"; even as he is sighing in his Gothic chamber, listening to the "rippling sound of the lake's billow, / With all the mystery by midnight caused," he is only "restless, and perplexed, and compromised." Byron has dropped the incest innuendoes, and Juan comes off so perfectly blameless in regard to his amorous adventures that one can only attribute our hero's nervous condition to his self-immersion in the powerful aura of superstition that surrounds the desecrated ruins. Juan's encounter with the monk, "The thing of air, / Or earth beneath, or heaven or t'other place," is given such comic-horror treatment that it seems a hoax, although Juan goes "Back to his chamber, shorn of half his strength." The narrator informs us that Juan's taper is "Burnt, and not blue," and, according to the rules of haunting-superstition, no malevolent spirit could possibly be present. Juan, however, does not seem to accept this evidence as any indication of the visitant's benignity, and he appears at breakfast distraught and imperfectly groomed for the first time in his career as a dandy.

The breakfast conversation, about the "Black Friar," is initiated by Lord Henry, but Adeline's perusal of Juan's reactions to her husband's ghostly tale would lead us to suspect that she could very well be the ghostly culprit:

> She looked and saw him pale and turned as pale
> Herself, then hastily looked down and muttered
> Something, but what's not stated in my tale.
> (16.31.1–3)

She could be playing with him, distracting him from his quest of Aurora; or, in psychological terms, since Juan refused to allow Adeline to settle his marriage match for him, she would be the destructive mother figure, as voracious and repressive as Donna Inez, attempting to control Juan's virility to her own ends. She becomes the prime suspect in the ruse as the narrator questions her motives in singing of the Black Friar:

> 'Twere difficult to say what was the object
> Of Adeline in bringing this same lay
> To bear on what appeared to her the subject
> Of Juan's nervous feelings on that day.
> Perhaps she merely had the simple project
> To laugh him out of his supposed dismay;
> Perhaps she might wish to confirm him in it,
> Though why I cannot say, at least this minute.
> (16.51.1–8)

Byron returns to the metaphor of hell in canto 16, and, when he does, Juan, as a result of the previous visitation, is involved and expecting the spectral encounter. He sits in his chamber, as he did the night before, save this time "Expectant of the ghost's fresh operations" (16.111.8). The door opens with "a most infernal creak / Like that of hell"

(16.116.1–2). Juan seems about to be engulfed by something dark and dreadful: "A single shade's sufficient to entrance a / Hero, for what is substance to a spirit?" (16.116.6–7). Like the legendary libertine from whom he sprang, who puts forth his hand to touch the stone statue of the commandant, Juan puts forth his hand, determined to touch the "stony death," resolved to pierce the mystery, brave and defiant with a wrath fed by fear. He puts forth an arm, but it touches "no soul, nor body, but the wall." He cowers. Suddenly, the ghost has "a remarkably sweet breath," fair hair, red lips, and "a hard but glowing bust"—it is "The phantom of her frolic Grace—Fitz-Fulke!" (16.123.7–8).

Within the dramatic context of the poem itself, this comic revelation is particularly effective in contrast to all the tension and terror that the legend of the Black Friar and the scenery of the Gothic ruins has evoked. Considering the format of the Don Juan genre, a female ghost seeking Juan in pleasure, as contrasted to the traditional figure of the avenging patriarch, is the final explosion of the myth that *malus animus* is unique to the *burlador.* The neatest reversal lies in Byron's setting up Adeline as the female figure most likely to be subverting Juan's strength: instead of the usual hypocritical, aristocratic, cold character, Juan meets damnation from the warm Fitz-Fulke. She is the one person in the English cantos whose "mind was all upon her face," who openly enjoys the "Tracasserie and agacerie." In linking Juan's last fall to such an apparently uncontrived appetite, Byron is intimating that any female, no matter how voluptuous, or openly flirtatious, is as destructive to Juan as the repressive, manipulative Donna Inez and Donna Julia, because women in general are the statues that warm, or become erotically animated, under his art, and their aroused sexuality then threatens to engulf Juan. These fears and fantasies seem particularly meaningful to Byron, because he can employ Juan to play the role of *cavalier servente,* create continuous escapes for his hero, as he remains bound to Teresa Guiccioli; perhaps, even more significant than the vicarious pleasure that Byron derives from Juan's escapes is the satisfaction and relief he would derive in seeing Juan punished.

The fragment of canto 17 is the end of *Don Juan*—Byron leaves his hero with nothing; the curse of the dissipated is only an absence of something:

> Which best is to encounter, ghost or none,
>   'Twere difficult to say, but Juan looked
> As if he had combated with more than one,
>   Being wan and worn, with eyes that hardly brooked

> The light that through the Gothic windows shone.
>   Her Grace too had a sort of air rebuked,
> Seemed pale and shivered, as if she had kept
> A vigil or dreamt rather more than slept.
>
>   (17.14.1–8)

The ultimate irony is that even when sexuality escapes the moral confines, and appears spontaneous, it is deadly.

This final stanza and the one below, which immediately precedes it
in the original manuscript, form an absolutely coherent conclusion to the
poem:

> But Oh! that I were dead—for while alive—
> Would that I neer had loved—Oh Woman—
> Woman—
> All that I write or wrote can neer revive
> To paint a sole sensation—though quite common—
> Of those in which the Body seemed to drive
> My Soul from out me at thy single summon
> Expiring in the hope of sensation.

In terms of dramatic unity, the stanzas represent the only possible resolution to the poem's overwhelming variety of verifiable paradoxes and
playful juxtapositions: together, they illustrate the fusion of the naively
innocent Juan persona and the cynically experienced narrative voice. The
description of Juan's dissolution echoes the narrator's desperate apos-
trophe to Woman. Juan's malaise is more than an elegant social disease.
His psychic depletion corresponds to the narrator's "Soul . . . expiring
in the hope of sensation." The narrator's howls about Woman's "single
summon" belong to Juan's mute encounters with female sexuality. The
speaking voice metaphorically articulates an awareness of the oedipal neurosis, which Juan has only been capable of acting out. The conflicting
fantasies and fears of engulfment are expressed in both stanzas through
Romantic expletives of guilt and anxiety. Fear and impotency are Byron's
concessions to his own psychic reality, and about as close as he ever comes
to a public statement of morality.

If one compares the merging of the narrator's emotion and Juan's
physical state in the last two stanzas with Byron's feelings about his role
as *cavalier servente* to Teresa Guiccioli, the oedipal conflicts of the poem
and the poet appear contiguous. In August 1819, distracted from con-

tinuing canto 3, Byron sent the following letter to his friend John Hobhouse:

> I have been excited and agitated, and exhausted mentally and
> bodily all this summer, till I sometimes begin to think not
> only "that I shall die at top first," but that the moment is not
> very remote. I have had no particular cause of griefs, except
> the usual accompaniments of all unlawful passions.

> I feel—and I feel it bitterly—that a man should not consume
> his life at the side and on the bosom of a woman, and a
> stranger; that this *Cicisbean* existence is to be condemned. But
> I have neither the strength of mind to break my chain, nor the
> insensibility which would deaden its weight. I cannot tell what
> will become of me—to leave, or to be left would at present
> drive me quite out of my senses; and yet to what have I con-
> ducted myself?

If adultery were the "unlawful passion" that tortured him, then the legal
negotiations between Byron and Count Guiccioli, in 1820, should have
eased the conscience of so infamous a libertine as he. Instead, the legal
agreement seemed to irritate. Like the legendary Don Juan, Byron hated
the rules and regularity of a contracted affair: "A man actually becomes
a piece of female property." Like his pantomiming hero and melancholy
narrator, Byron's engulfment anxieties, as expressed in this letter, out-
weighed "the recompense" of his relationship with the Countess. As
Teresa, herself, so aptly described the continuum of Byron's incestuous
delusion:

> How often has he not spoken of [Augusta] to me! and, much
> as I loved him, how often I was irritated by his tender affection
> for his sister! Augusta. C'était un refrain perpétuel.

No matter what shape the relationship with Teresa assumed, legal or
otherwise, or if the husband-father figure of the Count challenged or
sanctioned the affair, it was still, for Byron, "unlawful" or threatening,
and related to his sister-mother confusion.

Byron's separation from Teresa and the trip to Greece seem but
another sequel to Juan's adventures. For Byron, *Don Juan* was his psychodrama: using the Don Juan legend throughout, but making significant
alterations, he reshaped the myth in an attempt to confront his past

within the present of the poem. In [Jacob L.] Moreno's terms, all the characters in the poem are the "auxiliary egos" [*Psychodrama*] in Byron's own oedipal drama. Byron's Juan is not, nor was he intended to be, a hero: he is only the protagonist of the drama, the man in a frenzy.

Shipwreck and Skepticism: *Don Juan* Canto 2

Andrew M. Cooper

> *Life is, in itself and forever, shipwreck. To be shipwrecked is not to drown.*
> *. . . Consciousness of shipwreck, being the truth of life, constitutes salvation.*
> ORTEGA Y GASSET, "In Search of Goethe from Within"

Mazeppa, composed simultaneously with *Don Juan* canto 1 during the late summer of 1818, constitutes in several respects a preliminary version of the shipwreck episode in canto 2. In both cases a youthful adulterer undergoes a kind of descent into Hell, finally awakens before a Nausicaa, and thereafter remains exiled from his homeland. More important, Byron's active juxtaposing of different historical contexts in *Mazeppa* sheds light on his considerably subtler manipulations of ottava rima in *Don Juan. Mazeppa*'s opening stanza, alluding to the recent fall of Napoleon, introduces the poem as contemporaneous. The narrative, however, takes place immediately following the battle of Pultowa in 1709; and within that narrative, the old hetman tracks his "seventy years of memory back" to his "twentieth spring," 1660 (ll. 126–27). The time frames distance the reader from the events of Mazeppa's story, yet by forming a continuum they implicitly connect us at the far end. The effect is of a progressive historicism, as the intensely private experience standing at the core of the narrative (virtually a nonexperience, since Mazeppa loses consciousness at the nadir of his journey) is gradually subsumed into a public context, becoming transformed from, first, the original, near-solipsistic event itself, to the long stored-up memory of a single individual, to a

From *Keats-Shelley Journal* 32 (1983). © 1983 by Keats-Shelley Association of America, Inc.

beguiling story intended for a small "band of chiefs" (l. 44), to, finally, a poem whose audience includes ourselves.

Mazeppa thus appears less a formal poetic object willed directly by an author than a naturally evolved artifact inseparable from the surrounding contours of European history. Those contours, moreover, are seen to be defined largely by chance. *Contra* William Marshall, who ingeniously makes Mazeppa a parody of Charles's common sense, the narrator's position is not "clearly anti-providential," nor does Mazeppa express by contrast an "organized moral view of the universe" according to which his rescue by the Cossack maid constitutes a "providential intervention." Quite the opposite, the moral of Mazeppa's tale is that he was saved by an unforeseeable stroke of luck, the same luck that will perhaps save Charles now. In devising a clever torture for Mazeppa, the Count Palatine inadvertently raised him to power and so ensured his own defeat; by the same token, the defeated Charles may also live to destroy his enemies. The narrator's remark about "the hazard of the die" (l. 15) therefore tends to support Mazeppa's affirmation of chance as a positive force. If you have hit bottom, if the odds are "ten to one at least [for] the foe" (l. 114), then even random change can only help. This capacity to sustain ups and downs is what makes man more than merely animal, despite his untamed passions, which the wild horse plainly represents. Whereas the horse's unrelenting instinct for its homeland proves self-destructive, Mazeppa, whose home is simply wherever he happens to find himself (as shown in stanzas 3 and 4), survives his trek to love again. Similarly, the reason "Danger levels man and brute" (l. 51) is that it brutalizes man; but of course danger is not the sole condition of human existence, and hence Mazeppa ridicules Charles for making war to the exclusion of love (ll. 126–42). Indeed, the satirical thrust of his tale is its tacit advice that, since we all must suffer defeat sooner or later, it is better to have loved and lost than never to have loved at all and still to have lost.

Yet even random change has its limits; the dice may be fickle, but their permutations repeat. Thus the constant recurrence within the poem of rivers (the Borysthenes, the dark unnamed stream of fifty years past), horses (Gieta's, Mazeppa's Bucephalus, and the wild Tartarian courser), and an assortment of personal and military defeats suggests that, although meaningful causal connections between the individual occasions of experience may be impossible to determine, nevertheless life's various circumstances do unmistakably embody distinct patterns of contrast and resemblance. So the top and bottom of man's universe—paradise and death, love and brutalization—emerge from the narrative as fixed lineaments of experience without which it would lose self-differentiation and simply dissolve into the general flux. As random as an individual's life may be, it can never trespass those bounds beyond which lies the merely unimaginable: gods and dust.

Far more than even *Mazeppa, Don Juan* abounds with chance surprises, above all in the shipwreck episode of canto 2, where raw forces of nature solely propel the narrative. Subjugated by storms from without and starvation from within, man appears throughout the episode as a cipher lacking effective power to resist. A total newcomer to the larger world in which henceforth *Don Juan* takes place, Juan is here less a protagonist than just another sufferer scarcely to be distinguished from everybody else aboard ship. One recalls only his heroic stance, pistols drawn, before the rum-room (2.35–36), and his tacit refusal to eat Pedrillo (2.78). The shipwreck, then, is Juan's rite of passage into "our nautical existence" (2.12) on the sea of adventitious circumstance, the Deluge which precludes any direct return to Spain and Donna Inez. It serves to define the Stygian nadir of his new-found universe, much as the subsequent Haidée idyll defines its paradisal apex.

For Byron himself, moreover, it seems the decision to continue the poem beyond canto 1, apparently first designed as a separate poem like *Beppo,* involved an embarkation similar to his hero's. The two well-known stanzas he added to the completed draft of canto 1 make the parallel almost explicit:

> No more—no more—Oh! never more on me
>   The freshness of the heart can fall like dew,
> Which out of all the lovely things we see
>   Extracts emotions beautiful and new;
> Hived in our bosoms like the bag o' the bee.
>   Think'st thou the honey with those objects grew?
> Alas! 'twas not in them, but in thy power
> To double even the sweetness of a flower.
>
> (1.214)

"Thou" evidently refers to Byron's reader. Assuming our ignorance of the melancholy truth he wishes to convey, the poet rejects the earlier first-person plural and addresses the reader directly. Yet the continuing second person of the next stanza reveals that Byron is really addressing his own heart, perhaps has been all along:

> No more—no more—Oh! never more, my heart,
> Canst thou be my sole world, my universe!
> Once all in all, but now a thing apart.
> Thou canst not be my blessing or my curse:
> The illusion's gone for ever.
>
> (1.215)

Ultimately, however, such distinctions fail, for Byron's heart and his implied readers are one and the same. His heart can no longer be his universe, because it now must take account of the larger world outside itself, the world of concrete human life existing beyond poetry and encompassing ourselves as actual readers. Hence *we* become the objects out of which the disillusioned poet will extract new emotional sustenance. The series of contexts that *Mazeppa* deployed as a framing device, then, *Don Juan* canto 2 actively incorporates as a method of composition. The consequent relationships between Juan's occasion of shipwreck, the author's collateral expressions of skepticism, and finally the individual reader's subsuming experience of both, supply the subject of this essay.

Unexpected as it is, the shipwreck episode starts out open-ended. Anything might happen. Yet it is almost completely closed off at the other end, and Juan seems to escape through an orifice. This development stems from the way the law of attrition at sea logically works itself out: "Famine—despair—cold, thirst and heat, had done / Their work on them by turns" (2.102), to which one might add drowning, bad meat and delirium, over-exposure, and sharks. If the one doesn't get you, the others will. The form of the episode is therefore a vortex of diminishing possibilities. Juan's situation grows progressively more cramped and isolated as he moves from the Seville aristocracy to a ship carrying approximately 250 people to a longboat containing 30. Within the longboat, Juan's refusal to turn cannibal distinguishes him from "all save three or four" (2.78) who die anyway, leaving Juan the sole survivor. As the allusion to Dante's Ugolino suggests, cannibalism is the innermost ring of this Hell; Juan's solitary struggle with Ocean's "insatiate grave" (2.108) is the nadir; like Dante he squeezes through it and emerges into a new world, Haidée's island.

Byron articulates the descent as a series of small mishaps in which hopes are raised only to be dashed. The episode begins in full expectation of a safe passage; but then "at one o'clock" the ship is suddenly about to sink (2.27). Then it appears the pumps will save them; but then they almost capsize in a squall (2.30). Then there comes "a flash of hope once more" as the wind lulls with "a glimpse of sunshine" (2.38); but then the storm renews and the boats must get out (2.45). Then we learn that, as "'T is very certain the desire of life / Prolongs it," "people in an open boat [can] live upon the love of life" (2.64–66); but then we also learn that this will not suffice them indefinitely because "man is a carnivorous production. . . . He cannot live, like woodcocks, upon suction" (2.67). Then arrives a sleep-inducing calm that restores the survivors' strength; but then they awake and eat all their provisions (2.68). And so forth. The sequence suggests that events trick us into hope in order that we may be doubly defeated when they subsequently turn more dangerous yet. For the failure of each new promise of deliverance leaves the men not the same as before, but worse, because they have irrevocably used up one more chance for survival. "'T is best to struggle to the last," advises the narrator, "'T is never too late to be wholly wreck'd" (2.39)— good advice, surely; and yet three stanzas later one discovers its terrific irony, as the pumps give out and the dismasted ship rolls "a wreck complete" (2.42). It is as though the struggle to keep it afloat only led to a greater devastation (in fact, they deliberately cut away the masts to avoid broaching). This almost systematic way in which various saving possibilities only serve to become fresh defeats distinctly conveys the impression of an impersonal, casually malignant power of circumstance gradually revealing itself through the course of the episode.

Yet as their situation worsens, the men hope all the more intensely. From the cannibalism to Juan's final arrival on the beach, the poem presents a series of auguries: the shower of rain, the rainbow, the white bird, the turtle. The episode begins with an objective narrative of suspenseful action telling with considerable show of authority exactly what the ocean did to the ship and what the crew is doing to save it (2.27). The reality of the world "out there" is assumed; it may be inhuman and destructive, but one can still be confident of knowing how to handle an emergency. Later, however, the objective narrative virtually disappears— appropriately so, for no longer is anything taking place out there; inert, the survivors are not engaged in visible activity. The poem therefore shifts to a phenomenalistic presentation of their experience of reality, a realm in which belief, illusions, and symbolism play a vital part. Causality stands in abeyance; as the boat drifts, events seem to transpire without what Hume calls "necessary connexion," comprising instead simply an observed succession of independent phenomena (a rainbow, a bird, a turtle). In such a world, as in Coleridge's Ancient Mariner's, there is no reason for rational, purposive action because no likelihood exists that it will produce its intended effect. Mental activity such as hope appears at least as effective.

This is not to imply that the phenomenal world of the longboat survivors is experienced directly by the reader the way the Ancient Mariner's is. "We" are not in the longboat, "they" are: we see them through the narrative presentation. But this is just what we were *not* conscious of doing at the outset of the episode, when the narrative appeared objective. Now it is indeed a presentation and, moreover, a skeptical one. Says Byron of the rainbow: "Our shipwreck'd seamen thought it a good omen— / It is as well to think so now and then / . . . And may become of great advantage when / Folks are discouraged" (2.93). In their helplessness the survivors have made a possibly useful interpretation, no more or less. Byron's remarks are final, but they do not dispel our appreciation of how lovely the rainbow looked to "the dim eyes of these shipwreck'd men" (2.91). Their hope, which interprets natural phenomena as evidences of things unseen, is a tentative form of faith. Furthermore, the comparison of the rainbow to "Quite a celestial kaleidoscope" (2.93) suggests that such faith, under the circumstances, is inevitable. Like a kaleidoscope, a rainbow is not simply seen, but seen *into,* for it is an optical illusion existing as object entirely in the eye of the beholder. Being all appearance, as it were, the rainbow is thus whatever the half-dead men in the longboat perceive it to be.

If we prefer the narrator's skepticism here, it is with awareness that he stands outside the longboat and can afford to be rational. Standing in "their" shoes (which anyway they have already eaten), we might well find skepticism to be just one more discouragement. The point about the survivors' providential attitude is that it is more pragmatic than rationalism. They shrewdly anticipate a twofold benefit from the turtle and the sacred-seeming white bird: the animals are regarded as both auguries and meat, and the two viewpoints do not conflict. After all, given a boatload of starving men, how else is a turtle evidence of heavenly concern but that it may serve to sustain life? Similarly, what makes the bird a "bird of promise" is partly its promise of becoming food. Had the Ancient Mariner done the natural thing with *his* white bird—eaten it— he might have spared himself much grief, for the killing in that case would not have been wanton.

Such pragmatism gets its force from the way we experience the form of *Don Juan*'s ottava rima. Much has been said on this score, with attention usually directed toward the closing couplet rhyme. Alvin Kernan has emphasized the "but then" movement of the poem, its vital unpredictability; for him, the wave-like "onward rush of life" that the poem imitates, "upward to a pause, and then a sweep away, is most consistently present in the stanza form. . . . The first six lines stagger forward, like the life they contain, toward the resting place of the concluding couplet and the security of its rhyme—and a very shaky resting place it most often is." Edward Bostetter replies that the reader's expectations are not simply thwarted but renewed as curiosity; he proposes a complementary movement, "what next?" which "puts the emphasis on the anticipatory suspense." What perusal of the poem's individual stanzas shows is that these two movements coalesce so as to deny readers an accustomed complacency. We are drawn into and then thrust out of each stanza, which thus forms a miniature vortex. We end where we began, but meantime have become consciously aware of experiencing a fiction. Then we suspend that consciousness and proceed to repeat the process by moving on to the ever-imminent next stanza. The vortex form of the *Don Juan* stanza is not, however, simply a stylistic version of the thematic "falling" first discerned in the poem by George Ridenour; it is less the characteristic Romantic fall into reality or experience than a freely willed descent into a specifically literary self-awareness, into what both Jerome McGann and Peter Manning, borrowing a phrase from Wallace Stevens, term "the fictions of reality." "The actions of the poem complete themselves in [the reader's] consciousness," says Manning; yes, and they do so by directly exercising our moral imaginations. The questions Byron raises entail active examination of ourselves as social individuals. In canto 2 he is not asking, "What would you do if stuck in a longboat with thirty others without any food?"—as though unshipwrecked readers could give any answer that was not fantasy. The question lacks ballast; one wants to reply, "*I* would heroically save them all (but don't press me for details)." Instead Byron asks, "Exactly what *does* one do, having arrived at such a situation through force of circumstances?"—and what one does is, as usual in life, no one particular thing: not everybody eats Pedrillo. To repeat myself, "we" are not in the same boat as "them," but it is conceivable we could be because clearly their world much resembles ours. This consciousness of sharing the same context of possibilities as the shipwrecked men, without sharing even vicariously in their experience, is clarified by scrutinizing the individual stanzas themselves.

First consider stanza 27, the beginning of the end for all but Juan:

> At one o'clock the wind with sudden shift
>   Threw the ship right into the trough of the sea,

Which struck her aft, and made an awkward rift,
  Started the stern-post, also shattered the
Whole of her stern-frame, and, ere she could lift
  Herself from out her present jeopardy,
The rudder tore away: 'twas time to sound
The pumps, and there were four feet water found.

In poetry, the prototype for such a nautical *tour de force* was William Falconer's *The Shipwreck* (1762), an exciting first-hand account in which numerous professional-sounding marine terms are casually retailed in rhyming couplets. But Byron's stanza is effective as much by what it does not do as by what it does. It is all objective narrative, a sudden accumulation of events without any development. The wind shifts, and then no less than six violently active verbs happen to the ship one after the other; even the syntax, perfectly unextraordinary in itself, appears jerked about to fit the ottava rima. One realizes the helplessness of the ship, and the immense arbitrary power of the ocean that has evidently cuffed it. Appropriately, therefore, we find the birthday-snapper in the couplet rhyme is too damp to explode except matter-of-factly. Events have so overwhelmed the crew that it is not until line 7 that it manages to take defensive action; but even then, all the men do is discover still another way in which Ocean has anticipated them. So by forcibly failing to meet our expectations, this unusual stanza serves to reveal what, in fact, we expect of the usual *Don Juan* stanza: namely, that it begin with an objective narrative of events leading to description of an active human response, leading in turn to commentary by the narrator himself. Not coincidentally, this is the same pattern of development we saw take place within the episode overall: canto 2 moves from an impersonal narrative of the sinking ship implying confidence in the reality of the world "out there," to a presentation of the survivors' subjective construing of that world, to Byron's disinterested but sympathetic statements of skepticism.

    Stanza 50 I take to be the ottava rima model on which Byron elsewhere plays changes. It is a manipulation of narrative, but not to make any particular point. However, the manipulation involves several distinct shifts of perspective. We can enumerate them.

Some trial had been making at a raft,
  With little hope in such a rolling sea,
A sort of thing at which one would have laugh'd,
  If any laughter at such times could be,
Unless with people who too much have quaff'd,

> And have a kind of wild and horrid glee,
> Half epileptical, and half hysterical:—
> Their preservation would have been a miracle.

Lines 1–2) Objectively speaking, the raft is a futile effort. 3) So futile, the reader might find it ridiculous. 4) Now, however, we are grimly reminded that under the circumstances a raft is better than nothing. 5–7) And yet there is room for compromise between the two points of view: if you want to laugh, laugh with them, the hideous despairing drunks. 8) This line cuts off the lurid description of the laughter, itself slightly hysterical, by giving a blunt assessment of the raftsmen's chances. It thus repeats lines 1–2, only now it is the colloquial Byron speaking, not the impersonal narrative ("a miracle," not "little hope"). The stanza bends into the reader, challenging us directly with the "If" of line 4. Then, with the concessional "Unless," it turns back toward the fictive scene, which however now seems real in that it ironically subsumes our own response to it; with the introduction of "wild and horrid glee," the reader is forced to recognize that, under the pressure of actual shipwreck, his armchair amusement at the raft could well become something less pleasant. The intervention of Byron in line 8 completes the proof that we are not entitled to judge these people, only their chances for survival.

In the previous stanza, 49, the same pattern was used first to suggest the existence of an evil Deity hidden in matter, then skeptically to show that people aboard a storm-beaten ship at least have good reason to believe so. The first four lines, with their hint of a reversed Genesis, present the uncreating God of Byron's "Darkness." (What makes the last line of stanza 50 so potent is partly its suggestion that the raftsmen need *two* miracles, one to save them, plus one to create the good God who might bother to do so.) But then this vision is attributed to "hopeless eyes" looking only at "the night." Yet there is no cynicism here, for it next appears that the night these people saw really did "grimly darkle o'er the faces pale, / And the dim desolate deep." The horror they imagined therefore was not *all* illusion, a point the narrator reinforces by affirming that "now Death was here." The skepticism cuts too deep to be cynical.

Too deep, perhaps, for those who see in stanza 55 only a failure of good taste. Even Andrew Rutherford, author of the tough-minded "*Don Juan:* War and Realism" [in *Byron: A Critical Study*], hits upon this stanza as "the only one . . . in which Byron lapses into a flippant derisive tone which would have been perfectly appropriate in *Beppo* but which con-

stitutes a blemish, a breach of decorum, in his wonderful description of
the wreck."

> All the rest perish'd; near two hundred souls
>   Had left their bodies; and what's worse, alas!
> When over Catholics the Ocean rolls,
>   They must wait several weeks before a mass
> Takes off one peak of purgatorial coals,
>   Because, till people know what's come to pass,
> They won't lay out their money on the dead—
> It costs three francs for every mass that's said.

Certainly the lapse is there; yet in a sense it belongs as much to the reader
as to Byron. For consider the context. As early as stanza 34, the ship
presents the spectacle of a *Walpurgisnacht*: "Some plundered, some drank
spirits, some sung psalms / . . . Strange sounds of wailing, blasphemy,
devotion, / Clamoured in chorus to the roaring Ocean." The spectacle
intensifies once the sinking commences. We now become witnesses to a
microcosm revealing the various ways in which men prepare to meet
death: "Some went to prayers . . . / . . . Some looked o'er the bow; /
Some hoisted out the boats," "Some lashed them in their hammocks;
some put on / Their best clothes, as if going to a fair; / Some cursed the
day on which they saw the Sun, / And gnashed their teeth," "Some trial
had been making at a raft" (2.44–50). The ship sinks in a virtual apocalypse: "the sea yawn'd around her like a hell," "And first one universal
shriek there rush'd, / Louder than the loud Ocean . . . / . . . and then
all was hush'd" (2.52–53). Or almost all: wind and ocean continue, and
"at intervals there gush'd, / Accompanied with a convulsive splash, / A
solitary shriek, the bubbling cry / Of some strong swimmer in his agony." In retrospect, an instant and utter apocalypse would have been a
relief. Instead of anything so final, one ship went down. The point of
Byron's bringing in the agonized drowning castaway of William Cow-
per's poem here is to provide some distance from this disaster, which is
absolute in itself but limited; he shifts our perspective to the survivors
in the longboat (2.54).

   To read the limpid elegiac opening of stanza 55, then, is to prepare
for a eulogy: "All the rest perish'd; near two hundred souls / Had left
their bodies." The second phrase is taken as a pathetic restatement of the
first, recalling as it does the Ancient Mariner's "Four times fifty living
men" whose "souls did from their bodies fly. . . . / Like the whizz of my
crossbow." But it becomes a trick, for Byron proceeds, in a travesty of

Coleridge's literalism, to belabor theological assumptions hidden in the phrase. The result is a satire of the eulogy we expected. For plainly the "leavetaking" of these men's souls was not the graceful affair such a formula implies. After so horrific a spectacle, what remains to say? Only "cant." If we realize this, then the circumspection with which we read that "Nine souls more went" in the cutter will steady us to accept lines otherwise unacceptable:

> They grieved for those who perish'd with the cutter,
> And also for the biscuit-casks and butter.
>
> (2.61)

"High thought / Link'd to a servile mass of matter" is Lucifer's Hamlet-like description of man in *Cain*. Here the couplet performs the linkage.

We began this perusal with stanza 27, an objective account telling precisely what happened to the ship the moment the wind shifted. We end with lovely, allusive stanza 84:

> And that same night there fell a shower of rain,
>   For which their mouths gaped, like the cracks of earth
> When dried to summer's dust; till taught by pain,
>   Men really know not what good water's worth;
> If you had been in Turkey or in Spain,
>   Or with a famish'd boat's-crew had your berth,
> Or in the desert heard the camel's bell,
> You'd wish yourself where Truth is—in a well.

By contrast with meat, which must be hunted and killed, the rain shower comes spontaneously as a gift. Like Truth, water is valuable essentially; it is free, yet under the circumstances it makes these men "rich" (2.86). Chiefly, though, it is the biblical quality of the poetry that makes the rain so much resemble grace or manna. Lines 2–3 echo the thought that man is dust of the earth, his life a summer's day; there is a deep, melancholy sympathy for this fiery dust who feels his thirst so urgently. Almost immediately, however, this developing awareness of the boat-crew's universality begins to become rationalized by the philosophy of suffering introduced in lines 3–4. Line 5 goes a step further and addresses us directly; taking us outside the narrative, it establishes a global context for thirst in which "a famish'd boat's-crew" is but a local instance. Their predicament is not essentially different from that of others whose thirst we find small difficulty in imagining. The joke at the end becomes effective by our recognizing that it is our universal experience of water's preciousness that makes us identify it with Truth in the first place. This is the same pragmatism we met with earlier in the providential turtle. The allusiveness that functions as pathos in lines 1–3 thus becomes an explicit intellectual point in line 8—almost, but not quite, the butt of a joke. The rain shower *has* really seemed like grace; but it is no wonder that it should.

Clearly, Byron's skepticism is less a definite philosophic rationalism than a perpetual process of pragmatic adjustment. Hence it completes itself only in the reader's mind (not the narrator's, whose thought, however various, remains determined by what Byron actually wrote), as over and over we are made to confront, examine, and revise our own prior responses to the poem. To a skepticism so paradoxically thoroughgoing in its tentativeness, an affirmation any less indirect is bound to appear merely self-approving. As Peter Manning points out:

> *Don Juan* baffled contemporaries and incurred accusations of cynicism because its first readers did not realize that Byron had transferred the locus of meaning from within the poem outside to them. Pope draws his audience into a compact of solidarity against the fools he presents—the Dunces, the Timons, the Sir Balaams. In Byron, however, the object of satire is not a fictive, representative character, but the false assumptions in the individual reader that his reactions to the poem bring to the surface.

So with regard to the shipwreck episode, what is most striking about first readers' reactions is not their horror, but specifically their mortification, as though they felt Byron had personally duped them somehow. All protest their excruciated "consciousness of the insulting deceit which has been practised upon us. . . . Every high thought that was ever kindled in our hearts by the muse of Byron . . . every remembered moment of admiration and enthusiasm is up in arms against him"—thus the *Blackwood*'s reviewer. Keats—whom *Blackwood*'s held anathema—less prissily expresses the same sense of betrayal; in Severn's report he flung the book down, exclaiming that Byron had evidently grown so jaded "that there was nothing left for him but to laugh & gloat over the most solemn & heart-rending scenes of human misery; this storm of his is one of the most diabolical attempts ever made upon our sympathies." Such reactions are quite accurate in their way. Most of the stanzas just examined contain a development whose challenge to the reader could easily be construed as mockery or betrayal. As stanza 50 shows no less than 84, *Don Juan* elicits pathos not for the sake of pathos alone, but in order that we may consider its appropriateness within a particular context. Normally, this entails the intervention of the narrator whose irony, as in the stanza Rutherford singled out, can seem even to unmoralizing modern readers like the devilish laughing and gloating Keats imagined. Among contemporaries it appears that only Shelley, applying the arguments of *Areopagitica,* was able to grasp how the poem locates its meanings within the individual reader, thus making his response a direct moral act. "You unveil & present in its true deformity what is worst in human nature," he wrote Byron, "& it is this what the witlings of the age murmur at, conscious of their want of power to endure the scrutiny of such a light."

Byron's implicit rejection of the cannibalism, the aspect of the shipwreck it remains to consider, follows from the premium *Don Juan* places upon the socialized individual. That the cannibalism is to be regarded as a moral issue appears from the fact that somebody is killed. Nevertheless the reader is not allowed to pass judgment, and the narrator judges the event only by its consequences.

> 'T was not to be expected that [Juan] should,
> Even in extremity of their disaster,
> Dine with them on his pastor and his master.
>
> 'T was better that he did not; for, in fact,
>   The consequence was awful in the extreme;
> For they, who were most ravenous in the act,
>   Went raging mad—Lord! how they did blaspheme!
> And foam, and roll, with strange convulsions rack'd,
>   Drinking salt-water like a mountain stream,
> Tearing, and grinning, howling, screeching, swearing,
> And, with hyæna-laughter, died despairing.
>
> (2.78–79)

The "extremity" to which they resort is repaid in kind by the consequence being "awful in the extreme"; but holier-than-thou readers who believe the cannibals got what they deserve must immediately confront a mock-serious distortion of themselves: "Lord! how they did blaspheme!" The narrator here is holier than anybody, and as a result seems merely hypocritical: "Kill and eat people if you must, but swearing like that is an affront to society." Cannibalism thus appears as "man's worst—his second fall," the fall of civilized man into barbarism; the last two lines describe primarily the behavior of monkeys. This is Byron's societal ver-

sion of Coleridge's Death-in-Life. Yet the Ancient Mariner sucked only
his own blood, whereas Byron's boatcrew in much the same situation—
compare the calm at stanza 72 with that in *The Rime* part 2—choose to
sacrifice a victim to their vampiric surgeon.

Leading as it does to madness and "a species of self-slaughter"
(2.102), the cannibalism is seen to be a socialized form of suicide. Unlike
hope, "the desire of life [that] / Prolongs it" by binding "people in an
open boat" into a hardy little community (2.66), the killing and eating
of Pedrillo is an act of cynicism. It is the individual's capitulation to his
instinct for self-preservation at any cost, a desire of life murderous in the
event. In the boat the men "lay like carcasses; and hope was none, / . . .
They glared upon each other . . . And you might see / The longings of
the cannibal arise / (Although they spoke not) in their wolfish eyes"
(2.62). Like original sin, the longings arise and intensify from within;
motionless, the men are visibly regressing into barbarism (apparently
they have lost the power of speech); "like carcasses" is how they now
perceive one another. It would appear that Byron's survivors see only the
low half of what Lucifer saw, the "servile [and serviceable] mass of matter." Moreover, having consumed Pedrillo, "as if not warned sufficiently,"
the men next dispense with democratic lottery and like a wolfpack fix
upon the master's mate "As fattest" (2.80–81). Their dehumanization
emerges vividly in the next stanza: "At length they caught two Boobies
and a Noddy, / And then they left off eating the dead body" (2.82).
Previously the feast possessed a certain macabre gusto (2.77); now it
seems genuinely necrophilic, an impression heightened by the ensuing
reference to Dante's Ugolino. With the reappearance of normal food
sources, normal standards of edibility resurface, and the other meat is
recognized with horror as the damaged corpse of Pedrillo.

Cannibalism, then, represents the furthest reach from Spanish society, the barbaric inner ring of Hell below which lies the merely animal,
Juan's struggle with Ocean. In a parody of the Genesis God's prolificness,
Byron shows the survivors' day-by-day exhausting of their provisions;
finally on "the seventh day" (2.72), the day God created man and gave
him life, the boatcrew kills the Christly Pedrillo and consumes him. Yet
this Hell opens up within a group of ordinary, civilized Europeans. The
reader looks down into it from the circle of his own values, which are
the same—hence the encapsulated quality of the whole episode. The
cannibalism is barbarism localized as an unlikely but genuine possibility
occurring within a broader social context that, though it usually escapes
barbarism, nevertheless cannot control the force of circumstance that

makes barbarism always a danger. Pedrillo's skillful euthanasia by a doctor we may regard as Byron's *reductio* of a runaway principle of enlightened rational self-interest, his own Modest Proposal to the Malthusians in the audience.

Juan's heroism in the shipwreck is his Promethean persistence in civilized values that he knows, implicitly, to be greater than his own personal annihilation or suffering. "No! / 'T is true that death awaits both you and me, / But let us die like men, not sink / Below like brutes" (2.36), he tells the whiskey-craving crew, and silently proves his credo in the nasty crucible of the longboat. Unlike the others, he resists "the savage hunger which demanded, / Like the Promethean vulture" (2.75), the sacrifice of Pedrillo. For Byron, civilized man is a Prometheus who internalizes the vulture that gnaws him. Barbarism occurs when the individual looses his personal vulture to gnaw upon somebody else; inside and outside then merge, and the individual actually becomes his vulture. The cannibalism is Byron's literalization of this myth of the modern Prometheus; the bestial deaths that result, simply the natural penalty for so uncivil a "pollution" (2.75; the word translates the Aeschylean *miasma,* or blood-guilt, which as E. R. Dodd remarks, "is the automatic consequence of an action, belongs to the world of external events, and operates with the same ruthless indifference to motive as a typhoid germ") [*The Greeks and the Irrational*]. No matter then that "None in particular had sought or planned it," the cannibalism is inevitably self-defeating.

Admittedly, Juan's persistence may be ingenuous, but it reflects nonetheless a vigilant sensitivity to the possibilities for true, unspecious survival—that is, for Byron, survival "like a gentleman," without compromise. The change of mind whereby Juan finally eats his favorite spaniel shows not only that his forbearance of Pedrillo is something more than fastidiousness; it also attests his moral continence under even the most trying conditions. When it comes to the crunch, we see, the profligate Juan is able to make the crucial discriminations between the moral and the sentimental, the human and the merely animal, seeing which of them is inessential and expendable and which not. It is no coincidence that Byron's manipulation of his readers through the ottava rima involves us in discriminations of the same kind. Not that Juan is therefore a directly exemplary figure, but his behavior during the shipwreck does illustrate the same resolute pragmatism we discovered in stanzas 50–84. This we may summarize as follows. Hope for the best, and act accordingly, but do not expect this or that consequence to follow or you will soon despair. To doubt something, on the other hand, is not to believe it is impossible, but only unlikely; far from necessarily conducing to despair, every doubt thus contains in itself the hopeful germ of a possibility. Or as bold Mazeppa put it, the battle lost, his forces routed, and himself surrounded by an enemy "ten to one at least": "What mortal his own doom may guess? / Let none despond, let none despair." The shipwreck episode of *Don Juan* represents Byron's exploration of the ellipsis between these two statements, the first skeptical, the second affirmative, and his laying bare the moral fabric that connects them.

Chronology

1788	George Gordon Byron born, January 22, in London, to Captain John ("Mad Jack") Byron and Mrs. Byron (formerly Catherine Gordon of Gight).
1790	Mrs. Byron, her fortune spent by her husband upon lavish living, takes her son to Aberdeen.
1791	Captain Byron dies at thirty-six in France.
1792	George Gordon attends day school in Aberdeen.
1798	Inherits the title of his granduncle, the fifth Lord Byron ("Wicked Lord") and moves to Newstead Abbey, Nottinghamshire, Byron family seat.
1798–99	Tutored in Nottingham. Byron initiated into sex by a Scots maid, who also mistreats him.
1799–1801	Attends boarding school at Dulwich, near London.
1801–05	Byron attends Harrow School and spends his vacations with Mrs. Byron at Southwell.
1803	First romance with Mary Chaworth of Annesley Hall, grandniece of Lord Chaworth, who had been killed by the "Wicked" Lord Byron in a duel.
1804	Begins correspondence with his half-sister, Augusta.
1805	Enters Trinity College, Cambridge.
1806	*Fugitive Pieces,* first poems, privately printed.
1807	*Hours of Idleness* published. Byron is drawn into a Cambridge circle of young intellectuals and political liberals.
1808	*Hours of Idleness* attacked in the *Edinburgh Review.* Byron receives master's degree at Cambridge in July and moves to London.
1809	Takes seat, March 13, in the House of Lords. Publishes *English Bards and Scotch Reviewers* in retaliation against the

Edinburgh Review. Points to Pope and Dryden as the standards for English poetry. With John Cam Hobhouse he departs in July for a journey through Portugal, Spain, Albania, and Greece. Completes first canto of *Childe Harold's Pilgrimage* in Athens.

1810   Finishes second canto of *Childe Harold,* March 28. Travels in Turkey and Greece. Swims Hellespont, May 3. Lives in Athens.

1811   Returns to England in July. Mother dies in August.

1812   Gives three liberal speeches in the House of Lords. *Childe Harold,* published in March, brings immediate fame, and Byron becomes the darling of London's fashionable women. Affair with Lady Caroline Lamb.

1813   Begins affair in June with his half-sister, Augusta Leigh. Publishes first Oriental tales, *The Giaour* and *The Bride of Abydos.*

1814   Publishes *The Corsair* and *Lara.* Becomes engaged in September to Annabella Milbanke.

1815   Byron marries Annabella Milbanke, January 12. Hounded by creditors, he flies into frequent rages. Daughter, Augusta Ada, born December 10.

1816   Lady Byron leaves Byron January 15; formal separation signed April 21. Byron, on April 25, leaves England forever. Spends summer in Switzerland with Shelley, Mary Godwin, and Claire Clairmont, with whom he has an affair. Publishes canto 3 of *Childe Harold* and *The Prisoner of Chillon.* Begins *Manfred.* Travels to Italy.

1817   Allegra, daughter by Claire Clairmont, born January 12. Byron resides in Venice and engages in a liaison with Mariana Segati. Visits Florence and Rome; completes *Manfred* and works on fourth canto of *Childe Harold*; experiments in *Beppo* with colloquial ottava rima on the theme of Venetian life.

1818   Begins liaison with Margarita Cogni. *Beppo* published in February. *Childe Harold* 4 published in April. Begins *Don Juan*; finishes canto 1 in September.

1819   Meets Teresa, Countess Guiccioli in April, his last liaison. Spends fall with Teresa at La Mira and continues *Don Juan*; the affair is countenanced by her husband. Thomas

Moore visits Byron and is given the gift of Byron's memoirs. *Don Juan* cantos 1 and 2 published in July.

1820   Byron lives in Guiccioli palace in Ravenna. Continues *Don Juan*; writes first of poetic dramas, *Marino Faliero*. Teresa's application for separation from Count Guiccioli granted by the Pope in July. Byron visits Teresa at Gamba family villa at Filetto; becomes involved in revolutionary Carbonari struggle against Austrian rule in Italy.

1821   Carbonari movement defeated. The Gambas, Teresa's family, banished to Pisa. Outbreak of Greek war for independence interests Byron. *Don Juan* cantos 3, 4, 5 published in August, and Byron promises Teresa not to continue *Don Juan*. In September writes *The Vision of Judgment*. Joins Gambas and Shelley in Pisa in November. *Cain* published in December.

1822   British outcry against *Cain* and *Don Juan* increases. Teresa consenting, Byron resumes *Don Juan*. Leigh Hunt and family lodged in Byron's Pisa house. Shelley drowns in the Bay of Lerici. Byron joins exiled Gambas in Genoa. *The Vision of Judgment* published in October; British outcry excessive.

1823   London Greek Committee enlists Byron's aid on behalf of Greece. Byron sails in July for Greece; becomes severely ill after strenuous excursion to Ithaca. Sets sail for Missolonghi on December 30. *Don Juan,* cantos 6 to 24, published.

1824   Byron hailed in Missolonghi on January 4 as a deliverer. On January 22 writes "On This Day I Complete My Thirty-Sixth Year." Tries to form artillery corps to send against Turkish-held stronghold of Lepanto. Cantos 15 and 16 of *Don Juan* published in March. Byron gravely ill on April 9; incompetent doctors insist on repeated bleedings; dies on April 19. Mourned by Greeks as a national hero. Regarded throughout Europe as "the Trumpet Voice of Liberty," Byron is buried July 16 in Hucknall Torkard Church near Newstead.

Contributors

HAROLD BLOOM, Sterling Professor of the Humanities at Yale University, is the author of *The Anxiety of Influence, Poetry and Repression,* and many other volumes of literary criticism. His forthcoming study, *Freud: Transference and Authority,* attempts a full-scale reading of all of Freud's major writings. A MacArthur Prize Fellow, he is general editor of five series of literary criticism published by Chelsea House.

GEORGE M. RIDENOUR is Professor of English at the City University of New York. An influential critic of Byron, he has also edited Browning.

JEROME J. MCGANN is Professor of Humanities at the California Institute of Technology. An editor of Byron's poetry, he has written on Swinburne and on textual criticism as well as on the Romantics.

PETER J. MANNING is Associate Professor of English at the University of Southern California, Los Angeles. He is the author of a number of works on Byron.

MICHAEL G. COOKE is Professor of English and African and Afro-American Studies at Yale University. His books include *Acts of Inclusion, The Blind Man Traces the Circle: On the Patterns and Philosophy of Byron's Poetry, The Romantic Will,* and *Afro-American Literature in the Twentieth Century: The Achievement of Intimacy.*

CANDACE TATE resides in Victoria, British Columbia.

ANDREW M. COOPER teaches English at the University of Texas at Austin.

Bibliography

Beatty, Bernard. *Byron's* Don Juan. London: Croom Helm, 1985.

Beaty, Frederick L. *Byron the Satirist.* Dekalb: Northern Illinois University Press, 1985.

———. "Harlequin Don Juan," *JEGP* 67 (1968): 395–405.

Blackstone, Bernard. *Byron: A Survey.* London: Longman, 1975.

Bloom, Harold, ed. *Modern Critical Views: George Gordon, Lord Byron.* New Haven, Conn.: Chelsea House, 1986.

Bostetter, Edward E. Don Juan: *A Collection of Critical Essays.* Twentieth Century Interpretations. Englewood Cliffs, N.J.: Prentice-Hall, 1969.

Calvert, William. *Byron: Romantic Paradox.* Chapel Hill: University of North Carolina Press, 1935.

Clancy, Charles J. "Aurora Raby in *Don Juan:* A Byronic Heroine." *Keats-Shelley Journal* 38 (1979): 28–34.

———. *Lava, Hock, and Soda-Water: Byron's* Don Juan. Romantic Reassessment 41. Salzburg: Institut für Englische Sprache und Literatur, Universität Salzburg, 1974.

Cooke, Michael G. *The Blind Man Traces the Circle: On the Patterns and Philosophy of Byron's Poetry.* Princeton: Princeton University Press, 1969.

Diakonova, Nina. "The Russian Episode in Byron's *Don Juan.*" *Ariel* 3, no. 4 (1972): 50–57.

Doherty, Francis M. *Byron.* New York: Arco, 1969.

Eliot, T. S. *On Poetry and Poets.* New York: Farrar, Straus & Cudahy, 1957.

Elledge, W. Paul. "Byron's Hungry Sinner: The Quest Motif in *Don Juan.*" *JEGP* 69 (1970): 1–13.

England, A. B. *Byron's* Don Juan *and Eighteenth-Century Literature: A Study of Some Rhetorical Continuities and Discontinuities.* Lewisburg, Pa.: Bucknell University Press, 1975.

Garber, Frederick. "Self and the Language of Satire in *Don Juan.*" *Thalia* 5, no. 1 (1982): 35–44.

Gleckner, Robert. *Byron and the Ruins of Paradise.* Baltimore: The Johns Hopkins University Press, 1967.

Gunn, Andrew. "Don Byron and the Moral North." *Ariel* 3, no. 2 (1972): 32–41.

Jump, John D. *Byron.* London: Routledge & Kegan Paul, 1972.

———, ed. *Byron: A Symposium.* New York: Barnes & Noble, 1975.

Kahn, Arthur D. "Byron's Single Difference with Homer and Virgil: The Redefi- nition of the Epic in *Don Juan.*" *Arcadia: Zeitschrift für Vergleichende Literaturwis- senschaft* 5, no. 2 (1970): 143–62.

Kernan, Alvin. *The Plot of Satire.* New Haven: Yale University Press, 1965.

Lauber, John. "*Don Juan* as Anti-Epic." *Studies in English Literature 1500–1900* 8 (1968): 607–19.

Leigh, David S., S.J. "*Infelix Culpa*: Poetry and the Skeptic's Faith." *Keats-Shelley Journal* 38 (1979): 120–38.

Lovell, Ernest J., Jr. *Byron: The Record of a Quest—Studies in a Poet's Concept and Treatment of Nature.* Austin: University of Texas Press, 1949.

Manning, Peter J. "*Don Juan* and Byron's Imperceptiveness to the English Word." *Studies in Romanticism* 18 (1979): 207–33.

Marchand, Leslie A. "Narrator and Narration in *Don Juan.*" *Keats-Shelley Journal* 25 (1976): 26–42.

Marshall, William H. *The Structure of Byron's Major Poems.* Philadelphia: University of Pennsylvania Press, 1962.

Martin, Philip W. *Byron: A Poet before His Public.* Cambridge: Cambridge University Press, 1982.

McCabe, Charles R. "A Secret Prepossession: Skepticism in Byron's *Don Juan.*" *Renascence* 28 (1975): 3–14.

McGann, Jerome J. *The Beauty of Inflections: Literary Investigations in Historical Method and Theory.* Oxford: Oxford University Press, 1985.

——. *Fiery Dust: Byron's Poetical Development.* Chicago: University of Chicago Press, 1968.

Medwin, Thomas. *Journal of the Conversations of Lord Byron.* Edited by Ernest J. Lovell. Princeton: Princeton University Press, 1966.

Parker, David. "The Narrator of *Don Juan.*" *Ariel* 5, no. 2 (1974): 49–58.

Porter, Peter. "Byron and the Moral North." *Encounter* 43 (1974): 65–72.

Reeves, Charles Eric. "Continual Seduction: The Reading of *Don Juan.*" *Studies in Romanticism* 17 (1978): 453–63.

Ridenour, George M. "The Mode of Byron's *Don Juan.*" *PMLA* 79, no. 4 (1964): 442–46.

Robertson, J. Michael. "Aristocratic Individualism in Byron's *Don Juan.*" *Studies in English Literature 1500–1900* 17 (1977): 639–55.

——. "The Byron of *Don Juan* as Whig Aristocrat." *Texas Studies in Literature and Language* 17 (1976): 709–24.

Rutherford, Andrew. *Byron: A Critical Study.* Stanford: Stanford University Press, 1961.

Salomon, Roger B. "Mock Heroes and Mock-Heroic Narratives: Byron's *Don Juan* in the Context of Cervantes." *Studies in the Literary Imagination* 9, no. 1 (1976): 69–86.

Sheraw, C. Darrel. "*Don Juan*: Byron as Un-Augustan Satirist." *Satire Newsletter* 10, no. 2 (1973): 25–33.

Shilstone, Frederick W. "The Dissipated Muse: Wine, Women, and Byronic Song." *Colby Library Quarterly* 20, no. 1 (1984): 36–46.

——. "A Grandfather, A Raft, A Tradition: The Shipwreck Scene in Byron's *Don Juan.*" *Tennessee Studies in Literature* 25: 94–109.

Trueblood, Paul Graham. *The Flowering of Byron's Genius: Studies in Byron's* Don Juan. Stanford: Stanford University Press, 1945.

———. *Lord Byron*. 2d ed. Boston: Twayne, 1977.

Vassallo, Peter. *Byron: The Italian Literary Influence*. London: Macmillan, 1984.

West, Paul, ed. *Byron: A Collection of Critical Essays*. Englewood Cliffs, N.J.: Prentice-Hall, 1963.

Wilkie, Brian. *Romantic Poets and Epic Tradition*. Madison: University of Wisconsin Press, 1965.

Acknowledgments

"Introduction" (originally entitled "George Gordon, Lord Byron: The Digressive Balance: *Don Juan*") by Harold Bloom from *The Visionary Company: A Reading of English Romantic Poetry* by Harold Bloom, © 1961 by Harold Bloom, © 1971 by Cornell University. Reprinted by permission of Cornell University Press.

"'A Waste and Icy Clime'" by George M. Ridenour from *The Style of* Don Juan by George M. Ridenour, © 1960 by Yale University. Reprinted by permission of Yale University Press.

"*Don Juan*: Form" by Jerome J. McGann from *Don Juan in Context* by Jerome H. McGann, © 1976 by the University of Chicago. Reprinted by permission of the University of Chicago Press and John Murray Publishers Ltd.

"The Byronic Hero as Little Boy" by Peter J. Manning from *Byron and His Fictions* by Peter J. Manning, © 1978 by Wayne State University Press. Reprinted by permission.

"Byron's *Don Juan*: The Obsession and Self-Discipline of Spontaneity" by Michael G. Cooke from *Acts of Inclusion: Studies Bearing on an Elementary Theme of Romanticism* by Michael G. Cooke, © 1979 by Michael G. Cooke. Reprinted by permission of the author and Yale University Press. A shorter version of this essay originally appeared in *Studies in Romanticism* 14, no. 3 (Summer 1975), © 1975 by the Trustees of Boston University. Reprinted by permission.

"Byron's *Don Juan*: Myth as Psychodrama" by Candace Tate from *Keats-Shelley Journal* 29, (1980), © 1980 by Keats-Shelley Association of America, Inc. Reprinted by permission.

"Shipwreck and Skepticism: *Don Juan* Canto II" by Andrew M. Cooper from *Keats-Shelley Journal* 32 (1983), © 1983 by Keats-Shelley Association of America, Inc. Reprinted by permission.

Index

Los (*Jerusalem*), 67, 71
Lovell, Ernest J., 16
Lucifer, 7, 117, 120. *See also* Satan
Lyrical Ballads (Wordsworth), 64

Malthusians, 121
Manfred (*Manfred*), 65
Manfred (Byron), 46, 47, 48
Manning, Peter, 113, 118
Marchand, Leslie, 64
Marshall, William, 108
Mazeppa (*Mazeppa*), 107, 108, 122
Mazeppa (Byron), 53, 107–8, 110
McGann, Jerome J., 113
Medwin, Thomas, 59, 61
Mental Traveller, The (Blake), 70
Milton, John, 1, 30, 73
Milton (Blake), 1, 14
Moore, Thomas, 49
Moreno, Jacob L., 90, 105
Mozart, Wolfgang Amadeus, 3
Murray, John, letter from Byron to, 98

Napoleon I, 3, 12, 57, 107
Narcissus, 99
Nausicaa, 107
Newstead Abbey, 88
Newton, Sir Isaac, 11, 23, 24, 25, 80
Novalis, 69

"Ode: Intimations of Immortality" (Wordsworth), 5, 44–45
"On Seeing the Elgin Marbles" (Keats), 69
Original Sin, 23, 24, 25, 120. *See also* Fall of Man
Orpheus, 71

Palatine, Count (*Mazeppa*), 108
Paradise Lost (Milton), 30, 56, 72
Pasiphae, 60
"Peele Castle" (Wordsworth), 5

Pegasus, 19
Phenomenology of Mind, The (Hegel), 68
Philosophy of History, The (Hegel), 68
Plato, 73
Platonic tradition, 37
Polidori, Dr. John William, 69
Pope, Alexander, 1–2, 15, 51
Porta, Antonio, 16
"Prefaces" of Wordsworth, 35, 64, 81
Prelude, The (Wordsworth), 14, 30, 39, 44, 45, 72, 74, 78, 81
Prometheus myth, 4, 11, 12, 16, 25, 70, 121
Prometheus Unbound (Shelley), 1, 14, 68, 71, 72
Pultowa, battle of (1709), 107

Rape of the Lock, The (Pope), 2
Recluse (Wordsworth), 1
"Resolution and Independence" (Wordsworth), 72
Richter, Helene, 16
Ridenour, George M., 2, 3, 113
Rime of the Ancient Mariner, The (Coleridge), 120
Romantic poetry: and romanticism, 2, 5, 7, 14, 35, 38–40, 67, 69, 74, 81, 89, 113; concept of fragmentation in, 69–71; concept of infinity in, 69, 71–72, 75, 82; concept of order and method in, 67–68, 70, 75, 81. *See also specific poets*
Romilly, Samuel, 46
Rousseau, Jean Jacques, 16, 75
Rutherford, Andrew, 115, 119

St. Peter's Basilica, 81
St. Petersburg, 59, 60
Satan, 57. *See also Don Juan*; Lucifer
Schlegel, Friedrich, 69